PUFFIN BOOKS

THE AMAZING SP

CITY I

Challenged

There is silence for a mome … pider-sense starts buzzing, as the whirrin … engines catches your ear. A dark shadow mov … gainst the lights across the East River, and you see a bat-winged glider rise from the side of a courtyard overlooking the river. Swooping rapidly towards you is an all-too-familiar turbine-powered glider piloted by the Green Goblin!

How can that be? you wonder, stifling a cold chill that is tremoring up your spine under your Spider-Man suit. *The Green Goblin is dead!*

But you have no time for further questions. Your enemy is sailing over you, firing a blazing bolt of lightning-like energy straight at you!

Have you got what it takes to escape this sudden and vicious onslaught?

Roll one die and add the result to your Agility score. If the total is 11 or less, turn to **167**. If it is 12, 13, or 14, go to **191**. If it is 15 or more, proceed to **44**.

Whatever the outcome, only your decisions, and the luck of the dice roll, can help you find the maniac who is keeping the **City in Darkness**

MARVEL SUPER HEROES™

GAMEBOOK #1

the AMAZING SPIDER-MAN™

CITY IN DARKNESS

by

Jeff Grubb

Illustrated by Alan Kupperberg
and Keith Williams

PUFFIN BOOKS

To my wife and fellow comic fan, Kate, who managed not only to maintain my sense of humour while I wrote this, but also to keep her own as well.

PUFFIN BOOKS

Penguin Books Ltd, 27 Wrights Lane, London W8 5TZ (Publishing and Editorial)
and Harmondsworth, Middlesex, England (Distribution and Warehouse)
Viking Penguin Inc., 40 West 23rd Street, New York, New York 10010, USA
Penguin Books Australia Ltd, Ringwood, Victoria, Australia
Penguin Books Canada Ltd, 2801 John Street, Markham, Ontario, Canada L3R 1B4
Penguin Books (NZ) Ltd, 182–190 Wairau Road, Auckland 10, New Zealand

First published by Marvel Comics Group, a division of Cadence Industries Corporation 1986
Published in Puffin Books 1987

Printed and bound in Great Britain by
Cox & Wyman Ltd, Reading

FACE FRONT, TRUE BELIEVERS!

You are about to assume the role of the Amazing Spider-Man and encounter some of the most nefarious villains of the Marvel Universe in an exciting, totally new kind of role-playing gamebook.

Based on the popular MARVEL SUPER HEROES Role-Playing Game from TSR, Inc., MARVEL SUPER HEROES Adventure Gamebooks require only a single standard, six-sided die; a pen or pencil; a moderate supply of luck; and, most of all, your own personal skill in making decisions as you play the game. If dice are unavailable, a simple alternative, requiring only pencil and paper, may be used instead. See page 12.

MARVEL SUPER HEROES Adventure Gamebooks have been designed to read easily, without complicated rules to slow down the story. Once you finish reading the rules that follow, you should seldom find it necessary to refer back to them. Your choices are clearly stated at each choice point, with occasional reminders of additional options you have available.

Your adventure reads like a book, plays like a game, and offers a thrill a minute—with YOU as your favorite Marvel Super Hero!

YOUR CHARACTER

In this book, you are the Amazing Spider-Man—in real life, free-lance photographer Peter Parker. While you were still in high school, you attended a demonstration of the safe uses of radioactivity. At this demonstration, you were accidentally bitten by a spider that had been exposed to an extremely high level of radiation. The spider's venom intermingled with your blood, endowing you with the proportional strength and agility of a spider. In addition, you acquired a special "spider-sense" that warns you of danger, along with the incredible ability to cling to walls and ceilings.

Seeking to find a way to support yourself with your new special abilities, you used your knowledge of chemistry to develop a chemical webbing that, though easily applied, quickly hardens to a strong, flexible adhesive binding. So armed, you set out to make a name in show business, hiding your natural shyness behind a mask.

Your show business career was short-lived, however. After one early performance, you failed to capture a burglar, who later killed your beloved Uncle Ben. At that point, you learned the hardest lesson of your life—that with great power comes great responsibility.

Since that fateful day, you have fought evil and crime wherever and whenever you have found it. Your domain is high above the city, where you swing from building to building on your special weblines. You have battled many formidable foes. Sandman, Electro, Doctor Octopus, Vulture, and the Kingpin of Crime all count you as their enemy. You are feared by many, as a result of inflammatory editorials about you written by newspaper publisher J. Jonah Jameson. However, others have come to know you as a trusted crimefighter and a force for good in the world as you seek to protect the lives of the innocent. . . .

PLAYING THE GAME

The Marvel Super Heroes portrayed in this series of books have certain powerful abilities far beyond those of the average human being. As Spider-Man, your special abilities, which will allow you to attempt things a normal person wouldn't even consider, are listed on the removable **MARVEL SUPER HEROES™ Stats Card** located at the front of this book. The Stats Card lists everything you need to keep track of in order to play the game in this book. At the same time, it doubles as a handy bookmark.

SCORING

Playing the game requires that you keep track of three things—**Skill points, Karma points,** and **Health points**—on the Super Hero Stats Card located at the front of the book. An explanation of each of these follows.

HEALTH POINTS

Health Points represent your general health or life strength. If you are injured or become ill, you lose some of these points. If you lose all your Health points, you will fall unconscious and possibly even die. At any rate, if your Health points drop to zero or less, your adventure is over. If you are hurt or sick, you may regain some or all of your Health points by healing or by spending Karma, which is explained in the following section. Always remember, however, that it is not possible to regain more health points than you had at the start of the game.

Spider-Man begins this adventure with a total of 32 Health points.

KARMA POINTS

Karma points represent the effects your actions will have on your future. You earn Karma by doing heroic deeds, by making the right decisions, and in general by being a good person. Conversely, if you do things you shouldn't, you may lose Karma. There is no limit to the number of Karma points you can earn, but you will do better to spend your Karma than to hoard it.

You may spend Karma on any die roll you make to increase your chance of success. Here's how it works:

You must make your decision to spend Karma *before* you roll the die.

Once you commit yourself to spend Karma on a die roll, you *must* spend at least 2 Karma points. You may add as many more Karma points as you need to make your die roll successful, providing you have enough Karma points to spend. If you decide to spend Karma on your die roll but fail the roll because you didn't have enough Karma points to spend or because you chose not to spend that much Karma, you still lose the original 2 Karma points.

Karma may also be spent to regain lost Health points whenever you reach a choice point in the story. For every Karma point you decide to spend in this manner, increase your total Health score by 1 point. Be sure to subtract the same number from your Karma total. The reverse is not true, however. Health points may *not* be converted to Karma points.

Spider-Man begins this adventure with a total of 12 Karma points.

ABILITY POINTS

Ability points determine how easy or difficult it is for you to perform certain actions, called **FEATS**. Whenever you are asked to attempt a particular type of FEAT, consult the ability called for on your Super Hero Stats Card, roll one die, and add the result of the die roll to your Ability score. The text will indicate what you should do next, according to what your total was.

The abilities used in this gamebook are described below.

FIGHTING determines how good you are in armed and unarmed combat. Your natural skill, combined with your many years as a crimefighter, gives you a much better than average skill with your fists.

AGILITY is a measure of your coordination. The radioactive spider that bit you gave you the proportional agility of a spider, allowing you to dodge and leap great distances, as well as hurl objects with great accuracy.

STRENGTH determines how much damage you inflict when you hit something. It also tells how much weight you are able to lift. You have the proportional strength of a spider, allowing you to lift great weights. You often pull your punches, however, in order to avoid seriously injuring human opponents.

ENDURANCE measures how long you can exert yourself physically without resting. It also determines how well you can stand up to punishment, how long you can hold your breath, and how well you are able to resist the effects of knockout gas. Your Endurance is far beyond that of an ordinary human being—a definite advantage when you go up against powerful villains such as Doctor Doom.

REASON reflects how well you can solve problems with your mind. You have a college education, and you did some graduate work in chemistry before becoming a free-lance photographer, so you're no dummy.

INTUITION gauges how well you observe with your senses and are able to act on that knowledge. Your special spider-sense, gained from your encounter with the radioactive spider, helps make you aware of potential danger, even danger that you cannot directly see.

PSYCHE is based on your willpower and inner strength. A high Psyche score helps you to resist magic and mind control techniques. Your Psyche is far above average for human beings.

AGILITY WITH WEBBING is a special ability that is yours alone. You have developed an incredibly strong temporary adhesive that you can shoot from special web-shooters you wear on your wrists. Through long practice with these web-shooters, you are more comfortable using them than any other weapon. You carry extra cartridges of web-fluid in your belt, along with a mini-camera and a supply of spider-tracers, which are special devices that send out signals tuned to attract your spider-sense.

PLAYING WITHOUT DICE

Should you ever wish to play the adventure when dice are unavailable, there is a simple substitute that requires only pencil and paper. Simply write the numbers 1 through 6 on separate slips of paper and mix them up in a container. When a FEAT roll is called for, draw one of the slips, note the number, and place it back in the container. Mix the numbers up before you draw again. Each draw represents one roll of a die.

You, as Spider-Man, are now ready to face the dangers that lurk in the CITY OF DARKNESS. Turn to page 13 to begin your adventure. Good luck, and good choices!

1

You move through the brightly lit canyons of the city on a single strand of webbing. Below you the city is ablaze with light, from the powerful spotlights framing its most famous buildings to the soft glow of hundreds of street lamps and apartment windows. It is early summer and the warm weather has brought out most of New York's population. Couples stroll along the sidewalk, stopping to watch breakdancers and mimes. Executives out on the town hail taxis bound for the theater district. Street musicians sound out hot, muggy tones on saxes and clarinets, providing background music for the small-time hustlers plying the crowd with games of three-card monte.

You have a bird's-eye view of it all. Or in your case, a spider's-eye view. You swing down the street, high above the normal hustle and bustle, your weblines arching from their special web-shooters strapped to your wrists, providing a set of lines to carry you from building to building. You've got to get across town fast—a meeting with *Daily Bugle* Editor Robbie Robertson was supposed to start five minutes ago, and lateness is not a virtue looked for in free-lance photographers, not even when jolly Jonah Jameson was in charge.

Of course, you muse, *when it absolutely, positively has to get there overnight, Webslinger Express is the only way to travel.*

You hit a break between the buildings where your lines might not reach the next tall structure. Rather than risk missing a shot, you tuck into a roll, straighten at the last instant, and make a perfect two-point landing on a movie marquee.

"Hey, it's Spider-Man!" shouts a voice from the

crowd below. Heads turn and you feel the gaze of your admiring public.

"Wow!"

"Neat!"

"I thought he was from an imaginary story!"

"George, get out the camera!"

Ah, the tribulations of being a well-known, super-powered hero, you think, chuckling, *adored by millions, or at least hundreds, capable of stunts only dreamed of by mere mortals, in reality mild-mannered camera hound Peter—*

"Ya bum!"

The last comment breaks through your reverie and catches you by surprise. *Not the words of an admirer, even in New York City.* You scan the crowd below to see who your detractor is.

"Yeah, you, Spider-Bum! You're a menace to society! I read about it in the *Daily Bugle!* Jameson says you're a crook!" The speaker is a nondescript man, about thirty, wearing a tan windbreaker and a Mets' cap. You could pass him on the street without even noticing him.

Beneath your mask you frown deeply. *Okay, hero,* you think, *do you really want to take this kind of guff, or do you want to teach this loudmouth a lesson?*

If you're willing to put up with a little verbal abuse, go to **64**. If you'd rather deal directly with the lout, go to **45**.

2 The fire that rages from the exploding Octopus takes the better part of an hour to contain. You help the interns and orderlies evacuate most of the patients to safe areas and help extinguish the blaze. Gain 1 Karma point for your help—it would be more, but after all, you are responsible for the thing exploding in the first place.

The blond-haired intern in the loud Hawaiian shirt comes up to you holding the head of the Doctor Octopus you were talking to not long ago. "Alas, poor Otto, I knew him, Horatio, a robot of infinite jest." He tosses the head at your feet. "You know, I feel really silly about having tried to cure a robot of psychosis." Then he walks away.

You pick up the severed robot's head and look into its face. The cracked mask reveals circuitry behind it. All in all a masterpiece of robotics.

So they've been looking after a robot, you think. *This opens up possibilities.*

Turn to **137** and make another choice.

3

You activate the toggles of both web-shooters, spraying the entire room with a thick spray of your ever-trusty web-glop. You continue until a hissing noise at your wrists indicates that the web-shooters are empty.

Kraven, Mysterio, Electro, and Sandman are draped beneath the webs, while Vulture hangs motionless in the air.

Say what? you think. *This may be crazy, but gravity should be working, and a gummed-up Vulture should fall to the ground.* You see wires leading up from Vulture's frozen form into the darkness above. The figures are struggling within the webbing, but no one breaks out. *This is getting stranger by the minute,* you think, walking around the sticky mess to the far side of the room.

You check your belt and see that you have no more webbing cartridges on hand. *What a time to run out of gas,* you chide yourself.

[This means that you cannot use your webbing again for the duration of this adventure, and that even if the use of webbing is offered as a choice before you complete this adventure, you may not select it. Mark an "x" by your "Agility with Webbing skill."]

The door at the far side is a metal panel set back into the wall. There is a switch to the right of the door. Do you pull the switch (proceed to **153**), or try to break down the door (turn to **47**)?

4 "I agree," you say, your voice a tight whisper.

In dealing with this deadly enemy, you have gone against your own principles. Reduce your Karma to 0.

"I knew you would," says Kingpin, smiling and returning to his desk. "Actually, I am surprised that you sought me out for such a simple matter. Your trail begins where Electro was kidnapped—in the sewer itself. The trail should be quite clear. Follow it until it stops, and you will find the one who hates you more than I. Now, if you'll excuse me, I have some paperwork to complete. Please leave the way you came, and remember, I will call upon you for help in the future."

Like a robot, or a trained dog, you turn and leave Kingpin's sanctum. Behind you, you hear his deep, throaty laugh, the laugh of a man who has won a battle without having to take to the field. You leap out into the night sky and reflect on what you have lost this evening, and head for where Electro was kidnapped.

Move on to **163**.

With a well-practiced leap, you shoot fifteen **5**
feet straight up, reaching out to grab a handhold on the wall. With the other hand, you shed your loafers, allowing you to stand on the wall.

Below you, your would-be assailant is cursing a blue streak and wondering aloud where the heck you've gone. A devilish thought enters your mind, and, adhering a strand of webbing to your left shoe, you throw it down in the general direction of the cursing. There's a satisfying thump, and the cursing stops. Give yourself 1 Karma point for putting the mugger out of action for the duration of the blackout.

You change into Spider-Man from your position up on the wall and begin to scale the building. Go to **118**.

The Green Goblin sails over you and fires a **6**
bolt of lightning-like energy straight at you!

Make an Agility FEAT roll. If the result is 11 or less, go to **167**. If the result is 12, 13, or 14, go to **191**. If the result is 15 or more, go to **44**.

7 You bring your fists down on the solid concrete, and the great block shatters under the blow. Your aim is true and the ground opens, revealing a huge sewer system directly beneath the warehouse.

Andrews coughs on the dust and acrid smell that comes up from the sewer. "You could've TOLD me what you were up to!" he shouts between breaths.

"Look at it this way," you shout back, dropping down through the hole into the darkness beneath, "at least I found your dust." Grumbling loudly, Andrews picks a path through the rubble down behind you. Move on to **107**.

8 It takes you another twenty minutes to make it to the *Daily Bugle* building. Thirty-foot letters spelling out the newspaper's name dominate the forty-six-story building, illuminated by powerful spotlights. Your destination is the seventeenth floor, where the city room offices of the paper are located.

With a well-practiced flip of your body, you let go of your webline and, tucking into a somersault, land on the vertical surface of the building. Far below you, the New York masses hurry down Second Avenue without thinking to look up to see a man-sized shape scrabbling along the side of the building.

You make for the third window over, which you know leads to a convenient supply closet in which you can change back into your civilian clothes. *Miss Manners frowns on showing up for meetings in a crime-fighting suit*, you think, smiling beneath the mask.

The second window over is open, and voices come from the office within.

"Where's Parker?" says the first, a sharp tone made raspy by a continual diet of cigars.

"I don't know, but I've got a few other matters to attend to," says another more balanced, well-reasoned voice. There is the sound of a chair being moved away from the table.

"It seems that Mr. Parker's attitude toward time leaves something to be desired," says yet another voice, female, as a door closes in the room. "At least Sam's here. Let's get started." You move past the window, noting the voices mentally.

The first belongs to J. Jonah Jameson, publisher of the *Daily Bugle* and avowed Spider-Man foe; the second, Joe "Robbie" Robertson, the editor-in-chief; and the third, Kathryn Cushing, City Editor. She doesn't like you a whole lot either.

Wonderful. Robbie never mentioned that Cushing and Jolly Jonah were to be in on this meeting. Still, it has been a while since you've sent Jameson's blood pressure rising. Do you want to drop in on the meeting for a moment as Spider-Man, or pass on by to the other window?

If you want to spook Jameson, go to **125**. If you want to hurry up and get to the meeting as Peter Parker, turn to **96**.

9 You swing at the beast with your flashlight, missing it by the proverbial country mile. The beast, used to the dark, moves where your light is not, and you feel its teeth in your arm like so many sharp needles.

Letting go of the light, you bring your knee up against the creature's underbelly. There is the sound of air suddenly exhaled and the grip loosens. You've stunned the creature for a moment, and while it is regaining its bearings, you climb onto shore.

You take 10 points of damage from the alligator's attack. If your Health is less than 0 as a result of the attack, you pass out unconscious and are awakened later the next day by a search party. Your adventure is over.

If you are painfully aware of your sore arm, but otherwise alert, proceed to **100**.

10

Anyone who can turn off the lights in New York City has to have something on the ball in the first place. Trying to separate all the electrical and high-tech baddies and track them down may take some doing, but any job worth doing is worth doing over. You make a mental checklist of all the criminals who could pull off something of this kind.

First is Electro. Sucking all the juice out of Manhattan seems a bit much even for him, but who knows what those Pegasus boys and girls may have done to him by accident. Electro could be a piece of the puzzle, and he definitely does hate you.

The only problem is that Electro's trail ends at the far end of an alley.

Then there are such electrical villains as Shocker, who has turned up in blackout situations and has sparred with you enough to get a good grudge going.

This could be a giant-size illusion, which puts it in Mysterio's league. Two problems there: first, he'd have to convince the entire city there was a blackout, and second, Quentin Beck, in reality Mysterio, is in jail with Shocker and Lightmaster. *Or are they? With all the breakouts, I wouldn't be surprised if they are among the missing.*

Okay, so much for illusions and electricity. How about someone with the high-tech smarts to take this on? Doctor Doom is a possibility, but he seems to confine his grudge matches to the Fantastic Four.

Hobgoblin is another possibility, but a remote one. Challenging a foe to duke it out one-on-one in the middle of Times Square is more Hobby's style. And Hobgoblin always signs his notes.

Kingpin is out for the same reasons. This is too ornate for the Kingpin of Crime to think up. Kingpin would do something more subtle—like blow up the *Daily Bugle*.

Doctor Octopus is just smart enough and crazy enough to try to pull this thing off. He's scared to death of you, and he has threatened the city before in a number of exotic plots, such as putting poison in the ink of the *Daily Bugle*'s printing plant. Last you knew, he was under treatment in Brooklyn, but maybe it would be worthwhile to check him out. Some bad guys treat confinement like a revolving door.

And then there's Vulture. There's someone with a good technical background. Adrian Toomes hasn't been heard of for a while, and he has such a huge ego that he wouldn't think twice about threatening a city to get back at one man.

You throw a few more names around. Kraven the Hunter would consider causing a blackout dishonorable, so he's unlikely. Lizard has been cured. Sandman said the last time you met that he was going straight, and besides, this is too tough for him. Wizard and Trapster may hate your guts, but again, they hate the Fantastic Four even more.

Big groups such as HYDRA and AIM have been stopped by Spider-Man, but also by Captain America, Iron Man, and a host of others. Why pick on Spidey?

You shake you head. Names and faces dance in your mind, a ring of old foes laughing at you, daring you to take them on.

Turn to **197**.

11

Everything is dark, and the first thing that strikes you is the smell. *Just like the New York sewers. Phew!* Turning on your spider-beacon, you aren't surprised to find that you are, in fact, standing in a sewer channel that is nearly as wide as the warehouse above.

And I bet that this runs under the other warehouses as well, you think, flashing your light about. The ceiling (what remains of it) is dotted with red electrodes, some with unconnected wires still hanging out of them.

Neat trick, you reflect. *I'm not Reed Richards, but I'd say that those little babies are responsible for the missing equipment. They undoubtedly form a selective phase inducer, which lets nonliving solids slip through solids. The thieves never enter the building, and as such leave no clues. Except for the missing dust, which is phased through with the equipment.* The area is coated with a thick layer of gray over the muck.

Your light catches a shiny object, which you dig out and brush off—a foot-long, high-powered flashlight, more effective than your spider-beacon. You turn it on and the beam cuts the gloom more fully, revealing a path through the sludge. The path looks as if someone took a bulldozer through; it is an easy trail to follow.

The alarm gets louder and you hear footfalls and voices overhead. *Andrews has probably figured out that he's had another break-in. I can try to explain this, or head on. Maybe Andrews will listen and be understanding about a big hole in his floor. Maybe he won't call the cops. Maybe he'll help.*

You listen for a moment to Andrews, who is outside the warehouse, using a bullhorn to bellow orders to surrender.

"Naaaaaah!" you say to yourself, and start to follow the path through the slime.

Press on to **49**.

12 "Lemme guess," you say. "It's National Pick-On-Spidey Day. You know, when I was trying to figure out who was behind this mess, I never thought it would be a committee."

Your foes are strangely silent as they move in. *Best to hit them before they all converge,* you think. *I can reach any of them. Who should I trash first?*

If you want to get Electro first, go to **21**. If you want to attack Sandman, turn to **203**. If you want to leap up and get in a melee with the Vulture, go to **63**. If you feel that Kraven is the most deadly foe, go to **95**, and if you want to leap over Kraven and hit Mysterio, go to **160**. If you wish to use your webbing against all of your foes, go to **3**.

13

Great bolts of lightning-like energy light up the horizon to the east, stabbing out fingers of light against the darkened sky. The bolts hang for a moment, then the clouds ignite with a fresh energy that burns red over the darkened city. The energy forms words.

"*S-u-r-r-e-n-d-e-r,*" reads Sam.

"*S-p-i-d-e-r-m-a-n,*" you finish, sighing to yourself. "And your little dog, too," you add.

"Did you say something?" asks the writer.

"No. Do you think that's your answer? Where the power goes?" you ask.

Sam shrugs. The vendor mutters something about freaks making the city dangerous to live in.

"Whoever it is, he has a heckuva way of delivering a message." Sam wipes mustard off his hands. The flaming letters are already beginning to fade.

"I'd hate to be the wall-crawler. Look, the lights are coming back on."

Sam is right. The bulbs in the streetlamps are already glowing softly, the lights are flickering on up the street, and energy is returning to the city in an illuminated wave as the lights go back on, starting to the south and moving to the north, leaving the city as it was before: filled with light and life.

"Shall we be off?" asks Sam. "We've got an appointment, blackout or no."

You nod and follow him, wondering, *Who would hate me enough to shut down the power in Manhattan just to send me a message?*

Unfortunately, you realize the list is uncomfortably long.

Turn to **192**.

14 "Only one way to stop a naughty child," you say, ripping off one of the plates of the great machine, "is to take away his toys!" You reach in and grab a handful of wires.

The machine does not stop humming; in fact, its pitch becomes louder and more intense. *Wrong choice,* you think, looking up to see Doc Ock, now actively trying to control his machinery. The entire machine is heaving and pitching like a living thing, and fire and sparks are issuing from every seam. The whole ball of wax is just an instant from becoming an explosion that the Industrial Light and Magic would be hard pressed to duplicate. Do you attempt to save Doc Ock from the impending explosion, or instead try to escape yourself?

If you want to rescue Doc Ock, go to **74**. If not, turn to **136**.

15 You slip back to where you stashed your clothes and reappear moments later as Peter Parker. As you approach the group, they've opened the main doors of the warehouse, and Andrews is standing in the brightly lit opening, his arms outstretched, looking at the empty warehouse. You get an excellent picture of the security chief motioning toward empty space.

"Page one material," you whisper to Sam. " 'Portrait of a Man and his Missing Items.' "

"I was wondering when you'd show up," replies Sam. "Thought you'd gotten lost when Andrews stormed the door. I think he hoped to catch the thief red-handed."

"Anything to steal in there?" you ask.

"According to Andrews, it was filled with electrical lines on huge spools," says the reporter. "Just so much air there now. I'm going to hit Andrews up for a few explanations. Why don't you toddle off and get those pictures developed? I'll meet you back at the *Bugle*?"

You nod and head toward the entrance, pausing to snap a flash shot of Andrews yelling at one of his guards to search for other openings. Andrews is startled by the flash and turns on you, delivering a long string of unprintable oaths until you are outside the warehouse.

This is a chance for Spidey to do a little investigating on his own! you think, looking for an alley to change in. *Between this and Electro and our skywriter, I'll have my hands full. And I'm willing to bet one of Jameson's cigars that the three are tied together somehow!* Go to **111**.

16

You're in a scene that recurs frequently on Saturday morning cartoons: the hero is in the water, an alligator sneaks up behind the hero, the hero leaps out of the water and runs over the surface of the river to shore, the alligator right behind him.

You never thought that particular routine possible, but, standing on the shore, breathing heavily, you realize that you must have just given a pretty good imitation of it. Too bad there were no cameras to record it for posterity, only an albino alligator that remains in the water. After snapping at you a few times, the beast loses interest and swims away.

Ah, your mother is an attache case, you think triumphantly, as you look down the passage in front of you, turning every so often to keep an eye on the departing gator.

Reduce your Karma by 1 point for getting spooked by the gator. A dim light glows up ahead. Turning off your own light, you move down the passageway toward the glow. Move on to **165**.

17 " 'Consolidated Edison storage facility reports massive losses in the first quarter,' " you read aloud. " 'The Battery Park/South Manhattan number six storage facility reports massive losses through theft or unknown damage in the early part of this year. Neither the new head of the facility nor the chief of security has any idea how the materials are being transported out of the warehouses. The storage facility has been upgraded with additional bonded security guards, guard dogs, and electronic devices, but thefts are still occurring, including the theft of large items such as conductors, generator coils, massive spools of cable. . . .' " There seems to be quite a list.

"It's almost as if someone is trying to create his own electric company," says Sam.

"Can anyone do that?" interjects Kate.

"Not really," replies Sam. "Utilities are monopolies by charter, and every time there's a rate hike, there's usually some form of investigation. That's how these thefts originally came to light. No, I think whoever is doing this is working a black market of electronic gear, possibly selling it overseas, perhaps to unfriendly powers that are boycotted by our country."

"While the New York electrical consumers are footing the bill," grumbles Jameson.

You wonder at Jameson's sudden concern for the consumer. *Must own a large number of Con Ed bonds. Probably what got him on this case in the first place,* you guess.

Now Kate breaks in. "Sam has a meeting tonight with the head of security at Station 6. You're to go along to take some night shots, since most of the robberies occur at night. Keep your eyes peeled for anything that looks strange. This may be nothing, or it might be a widespread plot that the *Bugle* can expose."

"And *NOW Magazine* can publish in full," adds Jameson, "with your pictures."

"So make it good, Peter," continues Kate. "We can use your work. . . . Robbie?" she says, as the editor-in-chief comes through the door.

"This just came in over the wires," Robbie says, laying the message on the table. "Electro just broke out of a Project Pegasus transport a few blocks from here."

"Aren't the Pegasus people out of the super-bad-guy business?" asks Kate.

"For the most part, yes, but they have the facilities to move criminals like Electro from place to place. There seems to be a bunch of energy-type villains on the loose. News is out that Nitro has escaped again. Maybe there's a connection. We know that Electro had help on his escape. And, Jonah, Spider-Man was reported on the scene."

You steal a look at Jameson and note that the color is already creeping into his face. Another explosion coming. Time to exit stage right.

Kate slams her file folder closed. "Right. Let's get a man on the scene. Leeds, Urich, whoever is around. Parker, you go with Karpierz on Sam's warehouse case. I'll see if I can scare up another photographer to check the scene. I want to see your material by tomorrow, ten in the morning. Let's go." The city editor shoots you a glance that seems to say, "If I could trust you, I'd send you after the Electro story."

Nice job, Parker, you think.

Kate leaves the room and Robbie follows. You and Karpierz edge out, leaving a fuming J. Jonah Jameson behind. As you depart, you hear him utter a single name.

"Spider-Man!" He says it like a curse. You sometimes agree with that sentiment. Turn to **166**.

18 *First things first,* you think, scrabbling across the machine's sides to where Electro is held prisoner. The master of electricity howls soundlessly on the other side of a glass prison. Above you, Octopus is already starting to react. You see Doc's metallic arms reach toward you.

The bowl is designed for Electro's powers, not your spider-enhanced abilities. It shatters with a crash and a bolt of lightning erupts from the prison. You are flung violently backward and topple off the side of the machine.

"OCTOPUS!" comes an inhuman shout from the sphere. "YOU HAVE USED ME, OCTOPUS! YOU HAVE HURT ME! NOW I WILL HAVE MY REVENGE! I NEEEEED MY REVENGE!"

Electro emerges from the sphere, shining like a bright white beacon, throwing everything else into shadows. Ignoring you, Electro moves up the side of the machine toward Doc Ock.

Ock is ready, as well, two of his mechanical arms grabbing nets and weapons, while the other pair extend, carrying his body high above his opponent. Electro grabs one metallic arm, and a yellow glow courses up the arm to the mad doctor. Octopus howls in pain.

Uh-oh, the genie is out of the bottle, you think, watching the pair of them in their deadly embrace. The machinery they are fighting on is cracking, breaking apart. Do you want to try to separate the foes (turn to **74**) or escape before the entire operation blows (move quickly to **136**)?

19 You swing a few blocks ahead, and, one hasty phone call to Queens later, you intercept the reporter on his way to the Battery. If Sam is curious about how you got ahead of him, he doesn't show it. Go to **192**.

20 You sit on the side of a building and eat a late dinner, watching the excitement in the Con Ed supply area subside. Eventually the last police car pulls away from the site. You pitch your trash into a nearby dumpster (keep your city clean) and head over to the area.

You can try this one of two ways. You can

attempt to go in the front door and talk to Andrews, or sneak in and conduct your own investigation. Which do you wish to do?

If you want to try the frontal approach, go to **81**. If you want to sneak around, turn to **126**.

21

"I didn't think you were working on this alone, Electro," you tell your silent sparring partner, "but since you were the last one out of prison, you should be the first one back."

You know that a close encounter with Electro would be a close encounter with a living Con Ed plant, and that doesn't suit you. *With Electro seeming less than talkative and a little sluggish today, tripping him up shouldn't be too difficult. In fact, a little squirt of web-fluid in the right place should do the trick,* you figure. Moving quickly but carefully, you're right on target with your shot of insulated webbing. One sharp tug and Electro goes crashing—*CRASHING?*—to the floor. His right arm snaps off with a loud electric crackle, exposing an assortment of wires and circuitry.

Robot? What gives? you wonder. But there is no time to ponder, as the others are moving toward you in a predictably unified fashion, no doubt robots packing electrical charges not unlike Electro's. You run to the far exit where there is a switch and a metal door. Do you pull the switch (turn to **153**), or try the door (move on to **47**)?

22 You catch the taller goon on the chin, and he goes down like a sack of wet linen. He's out of the fight, so add 1 point to your Karma score. His partner, however, ducks at the last moment, dodging your blow. The force of your swing spins you around, and the goon ducks behind you. You feel the none-too-gentle pressure of a weapon barrel placed against your back.

"Real slow," says the goon, pushing the weapon hard into your spine. "We're going to walk outa here, past all those guards. If you want to live. You tell 'em to hold their fire, or I'll light you up like a Christmas tree."

"You picked the wrong hero as a hostage," you reply sternly. "Half the folks out there would just as soon shoot ME as YOU. Don't you read the papers?"

At the same time, you're thinking, *If I move fast enough, I can turn and take the gun out of his hands before he pulls the trigger. Or maybe I can leap up for that fire escape.* The alley is notably empty of things to use as weapons, other than a manhole lid lying at the far end.

The buzzing of your spider-sense pounds in your ears, and you realize that there's more danger here than on the range with a punk wielding a battery-operated cattle-prod.

You lunge backwards suddenly, bowling your attacker over.

"Stay down!" you bark at him as both he and his weapon clatter to the ground. You grab your assailant by the front of his uniform and toss him out of the alley.

At that moment, the alley explodes behind you, and you are lifted off your feet.

Turn to **55**.

23

The wound from the alligator's bite burns enough to make you suck in air through your teeth. You make a mental note to check it with a doctor later. Then, looking up, you notice that even without your light, you can see up the passage. There is a soft glow of light ahead. *Some super-powered villain working late?* you wonder, and limp in that direction to find the person behind the light.

Move on to **165**.

24

Great! you think. *The perfect place to change into Spidey, and I pick an alley already equipped with muggers!*

"Come on, mate," says the voice. "You can take the stuff out of your pockets or I can take it off your body. Have it your own way." There is a prodding of the knife in your back.

You can give the thief what he wants **(131)**, you can try to escape **(161)**, or you can attack the thief **(52)**.

25

Your strands of webbing are met halfway by the full force of the Green Goblin's handblasters. The blasters burn the web with a crackling force and sight of your opponent is lost for a moment in the resulting smoke.

Suddenly you see him again, moving at you through the smoke! The Goblin's face is twisted into a hideous mask of anger, and you have no doubt that he intends to plow directly into you.

Make an Agility FEAT roll to dodge out of the way. If the result is 15 or less, turn to **28**. If the result is 16 or more, proceed to **147**.

26 "Hey," says one of the workers looking up, "it's that spider-guy!"

"Spider-Man," you correct him, spinning and landing in front of the workers—three guys apparently on a coffee break. The speaker nods, a second workman looks surprised, while a third merely nods and bites into a jelly donut. "How's the work going?" you ask.

"Real mess down there," says the first workman, apparently the spokesperson for the group. "Looks like they had enough explosives down there to blow this whole block to the moon!" He chuckles at some private joke.

"Then I need your expert opinion," you say, leaning back against the generator. "If someone was down there a minute before the explosion took place, could that person have survived?"

"Hmmm," the spokesman rubbed his jaw. "I dunno, it's not likely. He'd have to move very fast or it would be zoom . . . bang"—the spokesman claps his hands together and motions to the heavens. The other two workmen grunt in agreement. "The passage is clogged in both directions, and it's going to take a while to dig a clear path out."

The sewers are closed off by falling debris, and anyone down there may have been caught in the blast. Would you like to check out the sewers (go to **155**), or try another option (go to **10**)?

27

The area outside the warehouse is a maze of light, with heavy-duty spotlights sweeping the walls of the suspect building. Below, the security men are calling in reinforcements and seem to have all the normal exits covered.

Which means I should cover the more exotic exits, you think, easily dodging the searchlights and keeping as much to the limited shadows as possible. In a flash, you are across the compound and on the roof of warehouse 12.

A searchlight beam passes by, and you duck. It hovers for a moment in your vicinity, and for a moment you are afraid you've been seen by some sharp-eyed watchman. Then the light passes on and you crawl up to one of the many skylights in the building.

You peer over the edge of the skylight into the brilliantly lit warehouse. The emergency lights, triggered along with the alarm, fill the warehouse with a brilliance that illuminates the scene in full, a scene that is every bit as troubling as it is impossible.

The warehouse is almost empty, and the last of an unknown number of mammoth rolls of electrical coils is sinking through the floor!

Go to **195**.

28

You cannot get out of the way of the plunging goblin glider in time, and both it and its passenger, who is still wearing a look of hatred, crash directly in front of you.

You throw up your hands to protect yourself from the blast, but it is too little too late. The force of the explosion knocks you off your feet, over the concrete railing, and into the sculptured bushes beyond, causing 10 points of damage to your Health. If your Health has been reduced to 0 or less by the crash, your adventure is over. You awaken in a hospital several days later, with a massive headache and a desire to get the number of that particular villain.

If you still have legs to stand on and aren't seeing double, turn to **194**.

29 You gently pry the grillwork from the window. Reduce your Karma total by 1 for breaking in. Octavius shows neither fear nor anger as you, his most hated foe, move into the room.

"Doc?" you say quietly, almost whispering.

Otto mumbles something about Dr. Jefferson, his analyst, but continues to watch you.

"Are you okay?" you ask, stepping toward him.

"You are Spider-Man?" he asks.

"Yes, it's me. I'm sorry about this, but I had to make sure you were all right." You feel terrible about being here—afraid you might push the little man deeper into his madness.

"Really, Spider-Man?" asks the figure.

"Cross my heart," you say.

"I'm supposed to tell you something," says Octavius.

"I'm listening," you reply. Small pinpricks begin to dance in the back of your brain. Danger?

"Boom," says Otto.

And the room explodes. Turn to **133**.

30 You walk up to the huge metal doors and grab them, wedging your fingers into the small space where they meet.

An electrical charge surges through you as you touch the doors. The shock is intense enough to override your own nervous system, so you cannot pull away. You are caught like a fly in an electrical web.

Makes sense . . . , you think, feeling the strength leave your body, *electrical bad guy, electrical trap . . . .* And with that your thoughts flee far away and the darkness of unconsciousness swallows you.

Your adventure is over. You may start the adventure again, subtracting 1 point of Karma from your starting amount to reflect the knowledge you have gained.

31 When you open your eyes, it looks like someone is spinning New York like a phonograph record. Two figures dominate the foreground. One is a Pegasus employee checking your pulse. The other is an officious-looking blond woman with her hair pulled back in a severe bun: the head honcho. The medic says something to her. She says something to you. She sounds miles away.

You shake your head, work your jaw, popping your ears. She's apparently waiting for a reply "Ah . . . come again?" you say weakly. The blast has knocked you loopy for a moment. Your Health is reduced by 12 points.

"I said, ARE YOU ALL RIGHT?" she shouts.

"Please. I'm deaf, not dead." You shake your head again, clearing the cobwebs. "What was the number of that truck?"

"Looks like the alley exploded. A bomb was pitched down the sewer; maybe that's where they stored their other weapons. You sure you're all right?" She looks torn between concern for your safety and anger about the blast.

"Just wonderful. My idea of a fun evening. Mind if I ask what they were after? Gems? Jewelry? Bruce Springsteen tickets?"

"Well, at least your sense of humor, such as it is, is intact," she sniffs, then turns serious. "We were transporting a prisoner from our upstate research facilities when we were ambushed. The kidnappers took Mr. Dillon with—"

"Dillon?" you interrupt, your heart suddenly in your throat. "You mean Maxwell Dillon?"

"Yes. You know him?"

"Know him!" you moan, suddenly angry as you realize who just slipped through your fingers. "I've made a career out of fighting him, but the moniker he prefers is *Electro*." Turn to **69**.

32

You push up against the ceiling, but it is like pushing into old cheese. The areas where you place your hands sink into the broken concrete, and the passageway fills with dust as the entire roof begins to sag and settle on top of you.

You see the workman watching you in horror. You shout at him, "Get back, and hurry!" Then you lose sight of him as you are completely buried by the falling concrete, dirt, and timbers.

Go to **134**.

33 "Doctor Jefferson, I presume?" you say, looking at the psychiatrist captive in the cell. It all fits together now—with five of the Sinister Six being used as lackeys, the sixth must be the head honcho. He must have put another robot in his cell to avoid suspicion.

The bespectacled man nods and puts a finger to his lips. He hands you a note.

The note reads: "He can hear but cannot see us. He has captured Electro and is using him to power a weapon to destroy you. There is a trap at the end of the corridor. Look up. Don't hurt him."

You look up and see a ventilator grill above you. You nod to him and, trying to make as little noise as possible, rip his lock out of the door. That complete, you give him an A-OK sign.

Do you wish to continue down the hall to the trap Doctor Jefferson warned you about (go to **108**) or use the ventilator shaft (turn to **138**).

34 You swing your arms back and feel a sharp pain in your left elbow as you connect, with a responding thud.

"Yeeoooch!" you shout, checking the knife wound on your arm.

The little so-and-so wasn't kidding about using his switchblade on me. If it weren't for my shirt and uniform, he'd have cut me worse. As it is, deduct 3 points of Health because of the wound.

You wriggle your fingers. It's painful but there's no serious harm done. Then you check your attacker. He'll ache worse than you will but he'll only be out to lunch for a short while Give yourself 1 point of Karma.

You hear voices coming toward you, drawn by

the sounds of the scuffle. Shedding your shoes, you amble up the wall and change into your uniform. Go to **118**.

35

The beast charges, its toothy maw wide open. It wants to be fed.

So you feed it the flashlight. Darting your hand into its jaws, you place the light business-end up in its throat. The gator tries to close on your arm, only to find its jaws propped open by the light.

It squirms away from you, trying to jar loose the object wedged in its mouth. The moment of distraction is just the time you need to get up on shore. You are short of breath, but you can still give yourself a point of Karma for defeating the alligator.

Hope he gets indigestion, you think, wondering what you are going to do now in the dark. Then you notice that it is not that dark after all. A soft glow behind you, up the passage where the trail through the muck leads, beckons like a warm fireside after a hard journey.

Warm fireside, my ears, you think. *Probably a hot time for whoever set this up*. You move toward the light and proceed to **165**.

36

You dodge out of the way at the last moment, as a massive bolt of electricity carves a massive gash out of the wall, just inches away from your camera. If you weren't sure before that the guys with the heavy artillery are the bad guys, that little bit of hate mail convinces you. *Not only are these fellows dangerous, they're downright unfriendly. Could it be they're friends of that loudmouthed Mets fan, or at least have been reading the same editorials?*

Your dodging drops you down to just above street level. One of the Pegasus guards spots you and waves you away. "Get back!" she shouts. "It's dangerous around here."

"Surely you jest!" you snap back. "It's more dangerous getting a cab when the theaters let out than this little garden party." You're too low to web up the bad guys without catching some innocent bystanders. Your best move would be to try to get between the two thugs.

You tense your muscles to leap across the street and move on to **92**.

37 You bring your fists down on the solid concrete and the force of the blow rings up your arms. A cry of pain escapes your lips and you take 5 points damage from slamming your relatively unprotected hands on concrete that will not give. If your Health has dropped below 0, your adventure is over.

If you are merely suffering from incredibly sore arms, move on to **174**.

38

You are hit squarely by the bolt from the mad doctor's machine, and the power of the entire City of Lights, Manhattan, surges through you. You are blessed that you lose consciousness. Your last thought before you do is that someone else will follow in your footsteps and deal with this deadly menace.

Your adventure is over. You may start again, using the information that you know, but reduce your initial Karma by 4 points.

39

As you walk out the door, you are aware of the darkness. Not just the night. The darkness. The street lights are out, their posts dark shadows against the darker store signs behind them. The buildings themselves rise like ebony towers to an overcast sky. The only light on the street is from cars, their headlights illuminating the sidewalks as they pass.

"What the heck!" says Karpierz, his mind no longer on the subway routes.

You turn to see that the lights behind you in the *Bugle* offices are dark as well. You can imagine the panic of people on the seventeenth floor, repeated in every building where people are working late—the cheery working environment suddenly plunged into inky darkness. A sudden fear creeps up your spine—a fear of being suddenly deprived of an anchor of security—the glittering lights of the city, staving off the night.

There is a quiet that lasts a single minute as you and everyone else in the city takes a breath and sees the surrounding darkness.

Then the noise begins.

Go to **135**.

40 *Discretion is the better part of valor,* you think, running for the window. You reach it before any of the thugs reach you. With your arms over your face, you leap through the closed window, out into the night air, about thirty stories up.

You fall ten stories, then catch yourself on a flagpole. Looking up at the thugs screaming for your blood, you think, *If Kingy ever strips his hangouts of flagpoles, I'll have to stop visiting him.*

Kingpin is not the man you want tonight, anyhow. Though he is a problem for another day. This night, however, your prey is the man who would darken a city to strike out at you.

Take 2 points of damage from your dramatic exit. If your Health is less than 0, you are in no shape to continue your adventure, and it ends here. If you are healthy enough for more action, go back to **137** and try another option.

41 Like a championship golfer shooting out of a sand trap and into the cup, you arch your web strands gracefully through the air. They hit the two goons dead on. *Hole in two,* you think. *Eat your heart out, Lee Trevino!* Add 2 points to your Karma score.

Man and weapon are securely stuck to the brick walls. You hear a cheer from the Pegasus people as you crawl down the wall to street level. One of the Pegasus guards, apparently the head honcho, rushes over to you.

"Why didn't you go after him? He's getting away!" she shouts at you, as if your mask interfered with your hearing.

"After who?" you reply, expecting, if not a burst of gratitude, at least a thank-you. "I come around the corner, find you street fighting with these rejects from 'Empire Strikes Out,' help you bag the pair, and all I get is grief!"

"Yes, you got those two," she replies, "but the other two got away with the prisoner!"

Prisoner? you think. *That makes sense. Armored car. Guards. Now some super-powered buggy-wuggy has been kidnapped. All in a day's work. Once more into the fray!*

A single bound takes you over the line of Jeeps and into the alley. You pass the two guys you've webbed up, their curses muffled under a blanket of webbing. The alley is empty, bare even of dumpsters, trash, and winos. *Hello. A proverbial open manhole. . . . Could it be that our shocking friends left so obvious a clue of their escape route?*

As you approach the manhole, your spider-sense begins buzzing. *Danger! Gotta get out of here!* You turn and head at top speed for the mouth of the alley. You are almost into the street when there is a powerful thunderclap of an explosion behind you. The ground erupts beneath your feet, and you are sent flying. Go to **55**.

42 Using a good deal of your non-insulative webbing, you create a battering ram at the front of the Hovercraft parked outside. Another two minutes and you have hot-wired the vehicle and are backing it away from the entrance.

You back up to where the trail crosses the stream, then throw the Hovercraft into high speed. The air whistles past you as the vehicle bears down on the doors.

"COWABUNGA!" you shout in a loud voice, jumping off the Hovercraft at the last possible moment.

The craft slams into the electrified doors at full tilt. Sparks dance off the webbing protecting the front of the craft. The door gives with a bone-shuddering crash, and the way is clear.

Score one for Yankee ingenuity, you think, walking through the now-open passageway. Give yourself 1 point of Karma for this smooth, though not incredibly subtle, move.

You step around the wreckage and go to **129**.

43 Moving carefully down the wall so as not to look like you are making any false moves or trying any super-powered stunts, you crawl down the wall to the waiting Karpierz, Andrews, and guards. You notice the security guards have their guns trained on you every step of the way.

"There's a good explanation for all this," you begin, but Andrews cuts you off.

"I'm sure there is," replies the security chief, "but I don't want to hear it. We're going to hold you for the police, wall-crawler. We've got some questions about missing supplies, and you are uncomfortably close to the scene of the crime. If nothing else, you're trespassing. We're going to take it easy, but no funny stuff. I don't even want to know who you are under that mask. Let's just wait for the cops."

As Andrews speaks, Sam is jotting down his words in a tattered notebook. *Probably thinks this is Pulitzer Prize material,* you reflect. *"The Day They Caught Spider-Man." At least Jameson will love it.*

Andrews is right. It takes an hour for an armored car to arrive to take you to the station, another hour for you to be processed—pictures but no prints; the police have a lot of problems on their hands with the blackout.

Then you spend two hours waiting for police questioning and an hour of questioning with a court-appointed attorney present. You tell them what you know. They press for more details. You cooperate as much as you can. Con Ed decides not to press charges. *Jameson would be pulling his hair out,* you think. Without a charge, you are finally free to go.

By that time, however, it's all over. As you leave the police station via the roof—there's a mob of reporters outside—you hear a radio report on a massive battle in which the criminal that was responsible for the blackout was caught by Daredevil and brought in.

It figures, you think, swinging away. *I get a polite evening of Twenty Questions with the police, and he gets the glory. Parker luck runs true to form.* You swing across the city, trying to figure out what you are going to tell Sam and Jameson about the mysterious disappearance of Peter Parker.

The adventure is over for you. If you wish to try

again, start again at the beginning, but with 1 less point of Karma than you originally started with because you know some of the pitfalls already.

44 You dodge the arcing bolt of lightning-like energy and, launching yourself off one of the concrete railings that ring the Plaza, leap up at your airborne attacker.

This can't be the real Green Goblin, you think as you sail through the air. *Even the original Green Goblin didn't have that much firepower in his glove-blasters.*

Somersaulting to avoid another blast, you make a perfect two-point landing on the goblin glider itself. "Hi, Gobbie," you say, taking a swing at your masked opponent, "I can't tell you how much you've been missed."

Make a Fighting FEAT roll. If the result is 8 or less, go to **102**. If the result is 9 or more, turn to **205**.

45 "Just great," you mutter aloud. "Not only do I get jumped by every two-bit villain that hits town, but now the peanut gallery wants to get in the act. Hey, Bonzo, how'd you like to see things from my angle?"

With that, you press the toggle located on your palm, sending a jet of sticky web-fluid over a nearby lamppost to hit and adhere to the collar of the loudmouth's jacket. You give a not-so-mighty tug, and the lout is raised up, eyeball to eyehole with you.

Your former attacker is not so loud now. In fact, he looks disturbed by the height, a good twenty feet of space separating the soles of his shoes from the pavement. You seem to have made your point.

"You were saying something about menaces," you prompt. The man only nods in mute agreement, his face ashen and covered with rivulets of perspiration. He works his mouth, but no sound comes out.

"Hey, quit picking on the guy!" a voice cries out from below.

"Look what he's doing to that poor man!" shouts another.

"He's a menace!"

Wonderful, you think. *You hassle one loudmouth and end up turning the whole crowd from admirers to hecklers. I should try to keep my cool.* Your verbal assailant is still gaping at you in shock, and you're suddenly sorry for losing your temper with the poor schnook. *This guy didn't do anything but repeat what he reads in the papers, and then I go and prove to him I'm some kind of monster.* Lower your Karma score by 1 point for this error in judgment.

The crowd is getting uglier, and you consider for a second leaving the loudmouth strung up. No, you're in enough trouble with the fans as it is, and Jameson would just write another nasty editorial. "Look, I'm sorry. Really," you say as you gently lower the man back to the pavement on the webline. He is still shaken and unable to speak, but he nods mutely as you let him down.

You are just about to swing off, hoping the crowd doesn't start throwing things, when you hear a muffled explosion nearby, followed by shots! The sharp reports of pistol fire are mixed with a strange, alien crackle that sounds like static electricity. Either a giant Persian cat is snuggling against glass buildings, or something unpleasant is up.

You resolve to make up for your earlier misjudgment and leap into action. Robertson and the *Daily Bugle* will have to wait. You follow the sound of gunfire to **146**.

46 "Okay, Sherlock," says Andrews, stalking into the middle of the empty warehouse, "who did it?"

"Elementary, Watson," you say, looking at the floor. "It was Professor Plum in the drawing room with the garden shears. Actually, how often do you dust in here?"

"Dust?" snarls Andrews, his eyebrows almost meeting as he scowls. "This is a warehouse! You think we have someone come in twice a week to tidy up?"

"No," you reply, kneeling and running your hands over the floor. "It's just that there should be a lot of dust here if this is a typical warehouse."

"So?"

"So whoever took the equipment took the dust as well," you say, as you stand up.

"You mean that our thieves were really collecting dust and accidentally caught a warehouse full of two-ton spools of wire by mistake?" Andrews's voice drips with sarcasm.

The disadvantage of wearing a mask is that people treat you like a lamppost and just about as bright, you think. You say, "No, only that the thieves removed the dust when they took your equipment."

"So how did they get in?" asks Andrews.

"They didn't," you reply. Andrews looks as if he is about to explode. You hold up a hand. "What is underneath this building?"

"Three feet of solid concrete," snarls Andrews, "without a single door in it."

"Doesn't have to be a door," you say. "Watch."

You swing back and strike the concrete with your fists. Make a Strength FEAT roll. If the result is 12 or more, go to **7**. If the result is 11 or less, go to **37**.

47

You put a shoulder to the door and bounce back as the plate sparks with electricity. You receive 10 points of damage to your Health. If your Health is 0 or less, your adventure has come to an end.

If you were only stunned by the warm tingle and still consider yourself among the healthy, move on to **199**.

48

You get about three blocks away before your conscience starts to bother you. *Here I go again,* you think, stopping atop a building, *running off on what may be a wild-goose chase while dodging Peter Parker's responsibilities. I told Sam I'd meet him at the Battery, yet here I go, off in the other direction. No wonder Parker's got a bad rep.*

Realizing you should honor your commitments, and reducing your Karma total by 1, you swing back to intercept the reporter **(192)**.

49 The path through the slime is uncomfortably smooth, clean, and recent in origin. You've gone about a mile underground before you realize what would cause it to be that way: a ground effects vehicle, or Hovercraft, traveling on a cushion of air. That cushion would push up the slime and debris as the vehicle passed.

You hear a chittering to your right, and swing your light to reveal a large rat, sitting on a pipe. The rat holds motionless for a moment, then squeals and bounds away.

Yuck, you think, *the last thing I want to do is meet up with ordinary vermin while I'm hunting down a real rat.*

The sewer passage widens and crosses a wider sewer, this one carrying a stream of dark water. The path of blasted algae crosses the stream and reappears on the other side, about twenty feet away, then disappears down another tunnel.

Ceilings too low to leap, you think, *and the walls are slicker than Jameson on payday. But it's either crawl or swim. I don't think they have limo service down here.*

If you want to swim across the stream, go to **115**. If you would rather try crawling across the ceiling, turn to **68**.

50 At the same time you shoot your webs, the goons in the alley notice you. Your webline is met halfway across the street by twin blasts of electric energy. The double blasts etch the evening sky with a sudden flash of brilliance, then all is quiet on the battlefield. You blink twice as the ghost images of the bolts fade from your vision.

Good thing my webbing doesn't conduct electricity, or else they'd be serving up Kentucky Fried Spider. You sigh, noting that the entire end of the alley is covered by the remains of your webbing. The two goons are standing in the alleyway, unharmed. *Well, at least I got their attention.*

Your spider-sense suddenly sounds like a cloud of angry bees in the back of your brain. The good news is that the guys in the hokey bodysuits are no longer firing at the people from Pegasus. The bad news is that they are firing at you!

Quick, make an Intuition FEAT roll to determine if your spider-sense has warned you in time! If the result is less than 12, turn to **59**. If it's 12 or more, go to **36**.

51 You are unable to get free of the plunging glider in time and you, your robotic opponent, and the glider plunge into the hard concrete of the UN Plaza. The firmly rooted flagpoles and statuary shudder from the impact of the blow.

You take 20 points of damage from the attack. If your Health is reduced to 0 or less, your adventure is over. You awaken several days later in a hospital and will require a long period of convalescence, even given your powers of healing.

However, should you still be feeling up to an escape from a burning glider, move on to **162**.

52 You reach for your pockets, as if to empty them out, then suddenly drive both elbows straight back, hoping your assailant's greed and the darkness has brought him close enough to strike him.

Make a Fighting FEAT roll. If the total is 11 or more, turn to **144**. If it's less than 11, go to **34**.

53 He sits like a spider in the center of his web. He looks more like a malicious spider than you do: he is fat, bloated, well fed on his power, corrupt. His web is made of shadows and concrete, the illusion of power and its reality. His reach is everywhere. He is Kingpin.

He is expecting you, of course. The meeting couldn't have been arranged without his consent. But you wish that you had been able to pick the meeting place. All the doors are locked except for the one at the end of the hallway. This stands wide open, and a dim light issues from within.

A trap? you wonder. *Could old Kingpin be behind all of what's going on? Or is the criminal mastermind playing his own game?*

You can still back out, turn and flee this sinister sanctum. If you choose to flee, proceed to **197**; otherwise, go to **189**.

54

The Vulture wheels into your path just as you leap into the air. Angling your body with precision, you bounce off of the winged opponent's back.

As you touch the Vulture's back, an electric shock runs through you. Reduce your Health by 5 points.

"Yeouch!" you shriek. *Since when has Vulchy started electrifying his suit? Unless our silent friends aren't who they appear . . .*

By that time, you are at the door. The door is another metal panel, with a switch next to it. Do you try to break down the door (turn to **47**), or throw the switch (check out **153**)?

55

You are lifted off your feet by the shock of the blast. The ground is shattered into a crazy quilt of broken asphalt. Make an Endurance FEAT roll. If the total is 11 or more, go to **121**. If it is less, turn to **31**.

56

As you start across the ceiling, you place one hand on a particularly slippery patch, and your fingers go skidding across the ceiling. You are overbalanced, and your other hand and your feet slip away from the roof. You fall into the water with a resounding splash that echoes through the passages.

So much for the element of surprise, you think. *At least I held onto the flashlight.* Fortunately, the water is only waist-deep where you've fallen. You pan the light about to see if you've alerted anyone to your presence.

Your light catches on a large, white object in the water, drifting toward you on the current. You think it is some part of a pier that pulled away until the forward section opens, revealing a row of sharp teeth. *Holy moly! It's a white alligator! I didn't think they were for real.*

This one doesn't appear to be aware that it is a mythical beast, however. In fact, it would seem to be intent on making you its next meal. You can try to run (go quickly to **90**), or you can stay and fight the creature (turn to **196**).

57 The mugger grabs your stuff and makes a break for the street, hoping to lose himself in the darkness and the crowds. As you start to change into Spider-Man, you reconsider letting him go, since there may be bigger fish to fry in the panic that is building.

Bigger fish to fry my eye! you think, reprimanding yourself as you slip your mask over your face. *It's letting the criminal go so I could do "better things" that resulted in Uncle Ben's death. If this crudbunny thinks he can use the cover of darkness as a mask, he's got another think coming!* You swing out of the alleyway after him, without bothering to don your gloves.

He's got a good head start, and he's trying to lose himself in the masses. Make an Intuition

FEAT. If the total is 14 or more, go to **127**. If it's 13 or less, turn to **85**. Oh, and reduce your Karma by 1 point for delaying so long.

58

You walk around the burning wreck three times as the fire dies down. What is left of the goblin glider and its robotic rider is scattered at the bottom of a shell crater, and radiating lines of black streak out on the concrete like a black sun painted by a street artist. To one side is the "arm" of the ersatz Goblin, still smoking. Give yourself 2 points of Karma for defeating the "Green Goblin."

You pick up the arm, turning it over in your hands. *My electronic wizardry is a little rusty,* you think, examining the massive electrical discharger located in the hand of the robot arm, *but it's dollars to doughnuts that this is a second cousin to what those goons that attacked Project Pegasus were packing.*

You hear the approaching sirens of the local forces of the law rising from the background din of the city traffic. *Great,* you think, *with my luck they'll haul me in for littering.* The idea of trying to explain to the police that you were in the UN Plaza fighting an enemy you thought was dead is singularly unappealing. Do you want to hang around long enough to search the rest of the area before the police arrive, or try another approach to find out who is truly behind this grim masquerade?

If you want to search the Plaza, go to **179**. If you would rather leave and try something else, return to **137**.

59 Your muscles tighten to leap clear, but the warning from your spider-sense comes too late. The corner of the building you are clinging to explodes in a massive blast of electrostatic energy. Lower your Health by 10 points, as you, your camera, and fifty pounds of brick go crashing to the sidewalk. Only a conveniently placed trash bin keeps you from becoming a spider-pancake on the sidewalk.

You pick yourself up from the trash, brushing a banana peel off your outfit. *Do Crockett and Tubbs ever have days like this?* you wonder, shaking coffee grounds off your sleeve.

"You there! Webslinger!" cries one of the guards from your side of the truck. "You here to help, or what?"

"I'm here to what," you reply as another bolt smashes into the building above you. *Devoted cusses, but bad shots,* you think. *Must be their first day out with their toys. Well, since the element of surprise is lost, there's always the direct route!*

With little more than a second thought of the danger you're putting yourself in by leaving the cover of the trash bin, you crouch, prepare to leap, and move on to **92**.

60

There is the sharp report of a rifle and the wall near your left hand shatters into fragments as the bullet smashes into the building. The shards of concrete strike you, inflicting 3 points of damage to your Health.

You quickly duck back into the nearest shadows and wait, your heart beating in your throat. You try to stop breathing as you hear voices below you.

"What was that?" asks one voice.

"I dunno," says another. "I thought it was a guy up there on the roof, but there's nothing there now. Nothing could have moved out of the way that quick."

"Musta been a cat or a squirrel," says the first. "This whole robbery shtick has everyone spooked, and we're probably shooting at shadows. I'll tell the chief it was a false alarm."

The voices fade, and a tightness in your chest tells you that you were holding your breath. You check the wound (more of a graze than anything else). Minor, but it hurts like the dickens. If your Health is less than 0, your adventure is over.

If you are still healthy, turn to **119**.

61

You look at the huge metallic doors. *Hinges on the other side. Probably locked. If I can get my fingers into the cracks . . .* Your spider-sense buzzes, indicating danger. *From what's behind the door? From the door itself? Maybe I should have stayed in bed after all.*

Do you want to force the door open (go to **30**)? Or would you rather try something more spider-like (go to **110**)?

62 "Now, wait just a darned minute!" you say, slamming a fist into the door. The door shatters into splinters, leaving the intern holding the doorknob assembly in his hands. The intern retreats backward to his desk. You follow him.

"I want some answers, and I don't want any runaround," you say, leaning on the desk the intern is crouched behind.

"Y-Y-Y-Yes, sir!" he stammers. "No runarounds. Ask away. Capital of Nebraska? Ship numbers on the *Enterprise*? How many times Liz Taylor's been married? I'm a whiz at trivia."

"Doctor Octopus," you say.

"Room 307. I really don't think you should go up there, though. He was making real progress before Dr. Jefferson left, and I think that seeing you might just set him back. Like into the Stone Age. But don't let that stop you."

You motion him to shut up. "Doctor Octopus IS here?"

"Yes," the intern gulps, "but please don't break

anything else. They'll take it out of my paycheck."

You wheel about and leave through the shattered entryway. *Wonderful,* you think. *I break down a door and threaten a man, only to find out that my prime suspect is resting comfortably upstairs. Talk about over-reacting.*

Reduce your Karma total by 2 points. You can go to **197** and think of something else, or you can try **206** to check out the intern's story.

63

You leap into the air, making for Vulture, who flies directly at you! The two of you collide in a mass of sparks, and you fall to the floor near your original location.

What is Vulture packing that lets him DO that? you wonder, picking yourself back up. The other opponents start moving toward you again. Go to **208** to check out the damage done and find out your options.

64

"According to the *Bugle,* I'm the Hulk's tailor," you shout back, already shooting out your next webline, "and if you believe that, there's this bridge I want to sell you." A ripple of laughter runs through the gathering crowd, leaving the heckler red and fuming.

Unwilling to spend a beautiful summer evening arguing with a heckler, you swing off, climbing the webline as you go. Give yourself 1 Karma point for keeping your temper in the face of adversity.

You get only about half a block away when you hear the loud, dull *whumpph* of an explosion nearby. The explosion is followed by the chatter of gunfire, mixed with an electric crackle that sounds like a high-school experiment gone wild. Robbie Robertson and the *Daily Bugle* will have to wait. Something has come up—something that may require the presence of your friendly neighborhood Spider-Man.

You kick into high gear and go to **146**.

65 Your arms rattle in their sockets as you strike the hard concrete with your unprotected hands. Take 5 points of damage because you bruised your hands badly when you made the blow.

You dance around the large divot you've carved in the floor, silently cursing the pain. In the background you hear alarms ringing.

Darn and double darn! you think. *I can't get down there, and now the guards are coming in after me. Stupid floor!*

You jump on the floor, hoping to spring up to the windows and escape. Instead, the floor gives way beneath your feet, and you plunge into the darkness below. Reduce your Health by 3 points as a result of the fall, and go to **11**. (If your Health has dropped below 1, your adventure is over.)

66 "Sam!" you shout over the rising din. "I've got an elderly aunt in Queens. If this blackout includes the boroughs, I'd like to make sure she's all right. How about if I meet you at the warehouse in about an hour and a half?" Sam says something that's lost in the noise, then nods and heads off down Second Avenue, carried by a wave of people. You duck around the corner into a darker than normal alleyway.

Hate to duck out on him, you think, unbuttoning your shirt in the dark to reveal the spider-symbol of your uniform beneath, *but I'd have a better chance of finding out what's wrong as Spider-Man.*

At that point, your spider-sense begins buzzing, and you hear the mechanical click of a switch-blade. Behind you a voice says, "No sudden moves. Just empty your pockets."

Go to **24**.

67

Argh! you think, mentally shaking off the power of the attack, *whoever this clown is, he has the original Goblin's finger-blasters beat eight ways to Sunday. Those things pack a real punch!*

You don't have time to question the attacker's identity further, though, as he is circling to make another assault. You can try to leap up to attack him, try to web him from the ground, or run from the battle. If you choose to leap up at the Green Goblin, go to **184**. If you want to use your webbing on him, go to **143**. If you choose to run, turn to **82**.

68 The walls are covered with gooey slime, as is the ceiling. As you reach the apex of the vault, you hit a patch of moss that must have been what primitive man used for Teflon. Make an Agility FEAT roll. If the result is 14 or more, proceed to **150**. If it is less than 14, go to **56**.

69 ELECTRO!

Early in your career as a webspinning wonder you first crossed paths with Maxwell Dillon, better known as the villainous Electro. A freak bolt of lightning transformed him from a lineman for Consolidated Edison into a master of living electricity, who promptly turned his newfound talents to crime. Each time he has gone on a rampage, you have hunted him down and caught him, and each time he has found a way to escape.

A wave of rage passes through you. To be so close and have him get away! Electro was never one to learn his lesson, or even to lie low. He'll be around, looking for revenge. And until he makes his move, you and the people around Spider-Man are targets.

"Spider-Man?" The commander of the Pegasus

security force intrudes on your thoughts. "I *would* like to thank you for your help. When these thugs recover, maybe we'll get some answers."

"Right," you say, shaking your head. "But by that time, Electro will be miles away."

She shrugs her shoulders. "We do the best we can, when we can. Look, these clowns are going to St. Arbogast's Hospital. Is there somewhere you can be reached when they come to?"

"I'll be around."

"Have it your way, then," she says, nodding, "If you have problems, tell them Captain Nash sent you." With that she turns away and starts shouting at her troops. "You men! Clear those Jeeps out of the way! Let's let those ambulances in! Blashfield! You and Lawson help set up the barriers. Have the police brass arrived yet?"

Just wonderful, you think, brooding. *Electro on the loose, and all I caught were a couple of small fry. To top it all off, Peter Parker is even later for that meeting. Some days, as the rabbit said, "You shoulda stood in bed."*

You leap atop the overturned truck, bouncing off its Pegasus emblem. At the high point of the leap, you let loose a single strand of webbing, mooring it against a handy flagpole jutting out from the Empire State Building, three stories above you.

Twisting your body, you swing up to the highest point, then fire another strand, and in this fashion swing off into the night, hoping to make it to the *Daily Bugle* before Robbie gives up hope on you. Behind you, the whine of police sirens and the shouts of Captain Nash are lost in the rest of the city noise.

Turn to **176**.

70 "I sail through the air, o'er the greatest of sleaze," you sing, leaping over your silent opponents. Vulture's attempt at interception is too late, but as he passes, you see metal strands running from his body up into the darkness. *Wires? Since when does that Winged Weirdo need wires to fly?* you muse.

You land at the other side of the room. The metal door is shut, but there is a switch to the right. Do you pull the switch or try the door? Behind you your foes turn as if controlled by one mind and move toward you again.

If you choose to throw the switch, press on to **153**. If you would rather try the door, go to **47**.

71 You walk right up to the front door of the South Brooklyn Psychiatric Facility and ring the bell. A sleepy intern answers, rubbing his blond hair and looking at you with half-opened eyes. He is wearing standard whites with a loud Hawaiian shirt underneath.

"This a pickup or a delivery?" he asks, yawning.

"I'm wondering about one of your patients," you begin.

"I have a few doubts about them myself," he

interjects. "Why don't you come back tomorrow morning when the doctors are here? You can lie on their couches and tell them about your long underwear."

"You don't understand," you say. "I'm Spider-Man. I'm looking for Doctor Octopus."

"Right," he says, running his fingers through his hair in frustration, "and I'm the Incredible Hulk, and I'm looking for Doctor Sampson. Come back when it's Halloween, okay?" He starts to shut the door.

You can use your abilities to show you are who you say you are **(116)**, you can show the intern you mean business **(62)**, you can try again as Peter Parker **(123)**, or you can check out the windows to try to locate Doc Ock's room **(206)**.

72

"Mind if I lend you a hand?" you ask, reaching toward the debris blocking the sewer.

"Don't mind if you do," says the workman. "I'll hold the light."

The debris is not as tightly packed as you first thought, and you quickly dig your way through to the other side of the rockfall. The ceiling holds, as well, and your companion follows you, flashing the light around as soon as you reach the other side.

The other side of the rockfall looks just like a New York City sewer. The slime on the concrete appears to have remained undisturbed for at least a few generations, and nothing is out of place.

"Blast," you say, your voice echoing down into the depths of the concrete pipe.

"You were expecting something, maybe?" asks your friend.

"Some clue. I had a hunch Electro escaped down here. There's another blocked passage behind us?"

"Yeah, but it leads to a dead end."

Do you want to try to dig through the other way? If so, turn to **79**. Otherwise, give up and go back to **10** and make another selection.

73 The warehouse is as empty as Aunt May's petty cash jar. There isn't even any dust on the floor, and the room looks as if it has just been swept.

Andrews looks as if he will have a heart attack. He's choking on his words as he answers some unheard question from Karpierz. "No, it's not SUPPOSED to be empty!" he sputters, trying to regain his composure. "It's SUPPOSED to hold fifty coils of wire, each weighing two tons. How does a hundred tons of wire just vanish?"

You are snapping pictures and examining the walls and ceiling. *No holes in either the walls or the ceiling,* you think. *Those wire spools are BIG. If they didn't go up or out, how about down?*

Make an Intuition FEAT roll. If the total is 14 or more, go to **105**. If it is less than 14, turn to **181**.

74

You haven't moved more than fifteen feet when the machine begins to spit fire and massive tremors shake the entire complex. You are thrown against a wall as the entire room caves in on itself, and you are immersed in darkness.

Only some time later do you come to. You see the city lights above you and inhale the fresh air gratefully. Doctor Jefferson, the madman's prisoner, is sitting by you, warming his hands on a cup of coffee.

"How long?" you ask, your throat feeling like you swallowed some dirt. You cough and try again. "How long was I out?"

"About an hour," says the psychiatrist, not looking up at you. "They found you among the wreckage."

"What about the others?" you cough again. "Electro? Ock?"

"No sign," the psychiatrist sighs. "No bodies were found. I wonder if they survived."

You sleep then, wondering if those two bad pennies survived, and when they will return to plague you again. For now, you have saved the city, and that is enough. Your adventure is over, and you have a well-deserved sleep.

75

You slam your fists hard against the concrete, and it gives way under your assault. A gaping hole appears where you struck the floor, and it quickly widens into an opening large enough for you to slip through.

Somewhere in the distance you hear alarms. *Better get a move on*, you think, and you drop quickly through the opening.

Go to **11**.

76 You find a likely-looking ledge nearby and, drawing your camera out from your belt, mount it firmly with a dab of webbing. You set the automatic timer to shoot the full roll at five-second intervals.

All these actions come automatically, smoothly developed over years of taking pictures of yourself in action. These pictures, sold first to Jameson and later Robertson at the *Daily Bugle*, have supplemented your income over the years, and now are your main source of ready cash.

You watch the unfolding battle and notice that the guys in the blue jumpsuits from Project Pegasus are taking a pounding from their attackers. There doesn't seem to be a lot of movement around the truck, one of those heavily armored monsters that the government favors, but fortunately there are no bodies, either. The guys with the lightning-firing bazookas look like members of HYDRA, but the green of their uniforms is too washed out and they are missing the distinctive "H" on the front. *Could some other flaky subversive group with bad taste in clothes have picked these outfits up at a rummage sale and decided to blow up government vehicles?*

Your fashion analysis is forgotten as your spider-sense, the super-powered sense that warns you of immediate danger, kicks into full gear. One of the goons in the alley has spotted you, and the way your spider-sense is buzzing tells you that he's got you lined up in the crosshairs of his weapon!

Make an Agility FEAT roll to get out of the way. Remember to add any Karma you wish before you make the roll. If the total is 12 or more, go to **36**. If it's less, turn to **59**.

77

The lights come on suddenly, blinding you for an instant before revealing a cavernous room with a single entrance at the far side. And before you stand five of your greatest foes!

Electro is there before you, blocking the far exit. Above him hovers the Vulture, beating his long wings to hover in place. Sandman, who has the ability to convert his body into sand, is to your right. To your left is Kraven the Hunter, holding a net, and behind the criminal sportsman is Mysterio, master of illusion.

Five of the Sinister Six, you note. "What's up, doc?" you say aloud.

The five move toward you without a sound. You can fight these assembled foes, you can run, or you can try for the far exit. If you choose to fight, move on to **12**. If you want to run, run to **120**. If you would prefer to try for the far exit, go to **177**.

78 Most of the windows of the South Brooklyn Psychiatric Facility are dark at this hour, but a few lights are shining as you approach—a few doctors cleaning up paperwork, or patients in need of attending.

Strange, you think, landing on the roof across from the facility. Doctor Octopus has always been my most deadly and persistent foe. We've sparred time and again, and he's always had some master plan to take over the city or the world or to defeat you. And because he has not been able to beat you, he is confined here. You almost feel sorry for the man.

From your perch, you examine your options. Ock's room is likely to be one of those on the third floor, judging from the heavy bars on that level. You could just bounce over there and look in windows, but no doubt you would surprise other patients, as well. You could try the front door, but there's little chance that they would let you in as either Peter Parker or Spider-Man at this late hour. What to do?

If you want to try the front door as Spider-Man, go to **71**. If you want to inquire as Peter Parker, turn to **123**. If you simply want to look in windows, turn to **206**.

79

The map the workmen have of the sewers shows a dead end on the other side of the blockage. *Which means that Public Works may just decide to forget about digging it out,* you note, *a perfect way for someone to cover his tracks.*

You start digging through the slime-covered debris blocking that passage. Your friend holds the light as you use your spider-enhanced strength to burrow.

You are about halfway through the blockage, and feel (relatively) fresh air on your face, when your spider-sense gives off a sharp warning buzz. Bits of plaster and stone begin to rain down around you. The passage's ceiling is dangerously unstable, and the whole works is about to drop on your head!

Make a Strength FEAT roll. If the result is 12 or more, proceed to **104**. If the result is 11 or less, go to **32**.

80

"Nighty-night, snooky-ookums!" you say, lashing out and catching each of the goons flush in the jaw. Their weapons clatter to the ground, and you're left the only one standing in the alley. Add 2 points to your Karma score.

So why is my spider-sense still ringing like a three-alarm fire? you wonder, scanning the empty alley. *Nobody else here. Not even any trash or trashcans. A suspiciously well-kept alley, except for that manhole . . .*

Your spider-sense shifts to a frantic pitch, and you realize the danger is from the manhole itself. *Something nasty's down there, and I don't think I want to be here to find out what it is!*

You leap straight into the air, reaching for a fire

escape ladder hanging twenty feet overhead. You are no more than halfway toward your goal when the shockwave of an explosion sends you flying even higher. The booming thunderclap comes from below, and the walls shake as flame jets out of the mouth of the manhole.

Turn to **55**.

81 You saunter up to the front gate and wave at the security guards. "Hi, guys," you say in a friendly tone. "You want to call your boss over here? I've got to talk to him. I *could* leap over the fifteen-foot fence surrounding this dump, but I want to do things the right way."

The guards look shocked (how often is it that a super-powered character comes wandering up and asks *permission* to enter?). One runs to get Andrews, while the other keeps an eye on you. He doesn't say anything, but he keeps his weapon handy. Add 1 to your Karma for trying the front door first.

In about two minutes, Security Chief Andrews comes huffing and puffing over to the gate. "What do YOU want?" he says, in a tone that questions why the earth hasn't opened and swallowed you whole.

"I'm selling Girl Scout cookies," you quip, noticing that Andrews's face is getting redder by the moment. "Actually I heard you've had a bit of trouble, and I'm wondering if I could help."

"Trouble? What trouble? We've just had a blackout that hit only Manhattan, a major theft that left no clues, and more police and nosy reporters than I care to think of. Now the heroes get into the act. Sheeeesh!"

"You *must* be Andrews," you drawl.

He stops and looks at you for a long moment.

"I have ways of finding things out," you say, hoping to answer the question in his mind. "Look, chuckles, you've got equipment disappearing faster than you can install it. You're up against something you don't understand. I'm offering to help you. You can turn me down, and I'll walk away, no questions asked. Or you can let me help you. If I get your thief, you get the credit and the equipment back. Whaddaya say?"

Andrews looks at you for a long moment, then motions the guards to let you in.

Turn to **46**.

82

When the going get's tough, the tough get going, you think, *to the Bahamas for a long vacation, for instance. I've got enough trouble with my living rogues gallery; now the dead ones are coming after me, too.*

Not looking back to see if the Green Goblin is following you, you dodge across the street. A few stray bolts mar the asphalt behind you, but no more of the thunderbolt-like missiles strike home.

You don't stop until you are half a block away, and then only to crouch behind a *Daily Bugle* paper dispenser to give yourself maximum protection in case the Goblin has followed you.

Looking back, there is nothing in the Plaza. You let out a sigh of relief, then chide yourself for your reaction. *Some hero. Sets out to find out who is behind it all, then runs like a scared rabbit when it turns out to be an old foe. Or does it? I mean, the Green Goblin is supposed to be dead. So what's he doing in the UN Plaza?*

A little more reflection brings up other questions. *Goblin always had a rich arsenal of weapons, yet this friendly chap just flew around and shot at me. Singular lack of imagination. Could it be that he was an imposter, created to rattle me? If so,* you admit to yourself, *he did a good job.* Reduce your Karma total by 1 point for being so spooked by the "Green Goblin."

The question is, hero, you think, *do you want to check out the area again, even if Greenie is there, or try another approach?* Since your chances of surprise are now nil, you decide that a quieter course may be better. Go to **137** and make another choice.

83 One of the little-known facts about SHIELD (Supreme Headquarters International Espionage and Law-enforcement Division) is that they are listed in the Manhattan yellow pages under "Government Agencies."

Twenty-five cents and five rings later, a chipper female voice answers the phone. "SHIELD headquarters, This is Debbie. May I help you?"

"Hello. I'm calling about the blackout."

"Yes?" comes the voice. "Do you have any information you wish to report?"

"Well, no," you say. "Actually, I'm looking for

information myself. This is Spider-Man."

A long pause follows. "I see," says the voice, a little more formal now. "And how can I help you, sir?"

"Well, I saw the lights in the sky. . . ."

"That matter is currently under investigation. As a matter of course, we cannot provide information on matters under investigation." The tone is now short and precise.

"I understand, but I was wondering if there was any connection between the blackout and AIM or HYDRA."

"I'm sorry, sir," comes the response, the temperature over the phone becoming chillier by the moment. "Such information is 'eyes only' and, as such, is classified. Now, if you will give me your real name, we could arrange an appointment for you—say, Wednesday?"

"But I'm on a case right now!" you say sharply. "The information will be useless in a couple of days!"

"I'm sorry, sir, but this is standard procedure."

You slam the phone down hard. *Blasted bureaucracy! I wonder if Captain America has these problems? I suppose if AIM or HYDRA is involved with this, I'll find out in due time—probably at the last moment.*

Turn to **197**.

84

You are checking to see if you have all your fingers and toes when one of the workmen says, "Will ya look at that!"

You look up and follow the beam of light through the now-open passage. By rights, the light should be trained on another concrete wall.

Instead, it plunges into the gloom of another wide, aromatic stretch of sewer.

The walls are coated with a thick layer of algae, but the muck on the floor has been churned up and pushed aside, as if by a huge push broom, leaving a path of clear concrete leading into the depths beneath the city.

Move on to **122**.

85 The mugger is quickly lost in the milling masses that have collected on the street. He could have dodged into any of a number of buildings, into the subway, or he could be right next to you, sizing up his next target. At any rate, he's gone.

And so is your wallet, with your identification, social security card, press pass, and ten bucks. Why does it seem that someone somewhere causes things like a blackout in order to get you personally?

You dodge back to the alley to finish changing into Spider-Man, making a mental note to report the wallet stolen. Reduce your Karma by 1 point, however. While ordinary folk confronted by an armed mugger should cooperate as much as possible, a super-human like yourself should have been able to deal with him in a nonce. At most, two nonces.

Change into Spider-Man and turn to **118**.

86

Knowing what awaits you (and not really happy about it), you leap into the room, dodging to one side, hoping that your lightning-like reflexes are better than his.

Make an Agility FEAT roll. If the result is 16 or more, proceed to **207**. If the result is 15 less, go to **38**.

87

You can just hear editor-in-chief Robbie Robertson saying, "I like your work, Peter, but the *Bugle* isn't in the business of publishing the webslinger's picture every time he fights some ordinary villains."

It's a terrible thing when two men with giant-size joy buzzers are considered ordinary villains. Must be inflation. Before Jameson became publisher, he'd buy anything to use in his anti-Spider-Man articles. "Spider-Man threatens trick-or-treaters," you imagine as a tagline for the pictures of this battle.

Anyway, you think, *engaging in my livelihood isn't going to help those government people trapped in that crossfire.* Another series of lightning-like bolts dances across the open space between the alley and the Jeeps.

The situation looks easy. Two goons, armed to the teeth, stand in the mouth of an alley across the street. You can't see if they have company behind them. You can easily make the leap and land between them, probably drawing their fire, or you can stay here and try to web up the pair of them.

Looks like a tricky shot, you think, *but I'd better make my move now, before they spot me. What's it going to be?*

If you want to leap into the alleyway between the two thugs, turn to **92**. If you want to try your webs, go to **151**.

88 Of Kingpin, there is no sign. *Probably went back to his penthouse by now, or off recruiting more hirelings to take me out. Now is the time for all good spiders to head for the hills. And to think I considered getting help from the sleazeball!*

You open the window and leave the room and its unconscious goons behind. Kingpin is another matter for another day. You know that he is not responsible for the crimes, and you have other fish to fry.

Go to **10** to reconsider your options.

89 You are blinded for a moment by the intensity of the lightning arching out of the river, or perhaps from one of the islands or platforms in the river. The bolts crackle and thunder with intense power as they lace upward over the city, literally burning words into the overcast clouds. The clouds writhe, and the energy from the bolts remain as glowing letters, like a celestial electronic ad in Times Square.

"SURRENDER, SPIDER-MAN," say the letters.

You look up at the sky, then look down, shake your head, and look up again. It still reads the same.

What next? you wonder. *A huge head rising out of the Hudson shouting, "I am the great and powerful Oz"?* Then the immensity of the situation sinks in. Whoever pulled this off is apparently responsible for the blackout, either to get the

power or to have an available audience or both. Someone who wants . . . you.

You go through a mental checklist of the people who would want you dead or out of the picture. The list is uncomfortably long. Before you, the lights are coming back on in New York as a wave of power moves from the northern to the southern tip of the island. The buildings slowly begin to glow, and the streetlights convert the rivers of light to more permanent bands of light and shadow. Things return to a state close to normal.

It looks as if Spider-Man isn't needed to find the missing power. And if someone wants you out of the way, maybe Peter Parker should be finding out why. Below you, you see the scarecrow form of Sam Karpierz pushing through the crowds. If I websling a few blocks, you think, *I can intercept him and have time to call Aunt May to tell her I'm all right. Of course, I could also ditch Sam and go Electro-hunting on my own. . . .*

Do you want to rejoin Sam **(19)** or strike out on your own to find the missing super-criminal **(48)**?

90 Make an Agility FEAT roll to see if you escape. If the result is a 14 or more, go to **16**. If the result is less than a 14, go to **142**.

91 A quick survey of the Plaza reveals nothing but the scorched remains of the pseudo-Goblin and his glider. The sirens are rising in intensity, and the police will be on the scene in a moment.

Come on, here, think, you tell yourself. *There must be something here to help. I was standing here, challenging my attacker (whoever was running the goblin), when suddenly, old GG appeared from the riverside. Ah . . . The riverside.*

You look over the edge of the courtyard and see an embankment running down to the East River. The embankment is generally nondescript, save for a large drainage pipe.

Drainage pipe? That's it, you realize, leaping over the side and crawling down the embankment. Behind you the first police cars squeal to a stop, but no one calls after you.

You scramble down to the pipe and look in. It's large, about man-sized and, from the smell of it, leads into the New York sewer system. At the mouth of the pipe is a small, powerful catapult-type launcher.

Bingo! you think. *The Green Goblin was launched from here and flung out over the East River.* Give yourself 1 point of Karma for finding the origin-point of your robotic attacker. *Now, the sixty-four-thousand dollar question: Is whoever is responsible for the launch from around here or . . . down there?*

If you want to check out the sewer further, go to **152**. Otherwise, return to **137** and make another choice.

92

Flexing the muscles that give you the proportional strength and agility of a spider, you leap into the fray. A bolt of energy sears across the street, blasting the wall directly behind you.

If I'd hung around there, I'd be a Crispy Critter for sure, you think, somersaulting over the line of Pegasus guards.

"Hold your fire, ladies and gents!" you shout, bouncing off the hood of the closest Jeep. "Perforating my uniform with lead violates its warranty and will mess up your civil service record something fierce!"

A blast of lightning-like force ionizes the air on top of the Jeep where you stood just moments before. Before the flash has dimmed you're across the street, directly above the goons.

"If I didn't know better, I'd say you didn't like me. You've been reading Jameson's editorials in the *Bugle* again, haven't you?" you quip as you drop down between them. "If you surrender now, I'll let jolly Jonah visit your cell."

"Eat Shock-zooka blast, Webspinner!" says the thug on your right as he fires a blast from his futuristic weapon.

"Shock-zooka!" you laugh, dodging the fiery blast. "You'd think that the people who invent these deadly gadgets would at least come up with original names! Sounds like something that attacked Tokyo!"

Before the thug can get in another shot, you rush him, grabbing the battery-operated bazooka and ripping it from his grasp. The goon on your left, a little dumpier than the other, watches in wonderment, muttering, "He moves so fast." The second goon seems so amazed by your speed he has forgotten to aim his own weapon at you.

"You guys are just slowpokes," you taunt, lashing out with both arms at the assailants, "and now it's nighty-night time!"

Make a Fighting FEAT roll. If the total is 8 or less, go to **109**. If it's 9, 10, or 11, turn to **22**. If it's 12 or more, go to **80**. Remember to add any Karma you may wish to use before you make the roll.

93 Make a Reason FEAT roll. If the result is 9 or more, go to **42**. If it is less than 9, go to **186**.

94 Ryker's Island is not the most accessible location in New York, and the Metro Tour buses usually just note its presence in passing on the highway. No roads lead to the rocky island, and the only way on or off is by water or air. This suits the city fathers fine, since Ryker's Island is home to a maximum security prison.

It takes you an hour to reach the island, first

hitching a ride on a passing tug, then snaring the underside of a police patrol chopper with your webbing. It takes another fifteen minutes to convince the guards at the front gate you are who you say you are, your intentions are honorable, and there are no outstanding warrants for your arrest.

"You know there are those who think you should be in this institution as well as the others," says the warden, walking around his desk.

"A sympathy you do not agree with, I take it," you reply, glancing around the office. Very comfortable, save for the bars on the windows.

The warden gestures with both hands, palms upward, shoulders shrugging. *What can I do?* the motion seems to say.

"I do appreciate the fact that you've agreed to see me at this late hour, and on such short notice," you add.

Another shrug. "I was up anyway. Ryker's Island is on a separate set of power lines than Manhattan, so we weren't affected by the blackout, but whenever there's an emergency, the inmates get uncomfortable. . . ." His words trail off and he looks through the grillwork of his office window over the prison yard.

You clear your throat. "About those prisoners . . ."

"Right. The prisoners." He opens a folder on his desk. Who in particular were you interested in?

"Lightmaster, Mysterio, and Shocker. They're all supposed to be inmates here."

"All right, let's see." The warden flips through his folder. "Dr. Edward Lansky, also known as Lightmaster. Quentin Beck, alias Ludwig Rinehart, alias Mysterio. Shocker . . ." The warden checks under his entry. "They're all present and accounted for, Spider-Man. Sorry."

You sigh. "Better in here than on the loose. I had to check." The warden nods and begins to walk you to the door.

"We can keep inmates like Lansky and the rest because they derive their abilities from the outfits they wear," says the warden. "Real super-powered individuals have been moved to other facilities. We just can't keep anyone from the Brotherhood of Evil Mutants here anymore."

"Or a Spider-Man," you interject as the warden walks you out.

The warden stops and shrugs again.

The warden is kind enough to offer you transportation back to Manhattan, though the chopper pilot assigned the task is less than pleased and says scarcely more than two words on the flight back. It's just as well, because you are deep in thought. *This has been a chase down a rabbit hole. If one of my old cronies had busted out, it would have been in the news. What now?*

Reduce your Karma by 1 point and go to **197**.

95 *Let's hit the weakest members first,* you think, dodging to the left where Kraven and Mysterio are. *I'll use Kraven as a missile against Vulture, then bowl over Mysterio . . .*

Your thinking stops right there as you ram into Kraven with your shoulder. Go to **208** to find out what damage has been done.

96 The storage closet is empty, and you quickly slip through the open window. *Who locks windows seventeen stories up?* A quick change later and Peter Parker, boy photographer, emerges quietly into the city room, heading for the conference room where Jameson and Cushing were just discussing your relative merits.

"You're late," says Robbie, parked outside the conference room door loading his pipe. City Editor Cushing has no tolerance for smoking, so both Jonah and Robbie have taken to sneaking smokes when not in her presence.

"Sorry, Robbie, I just got caught in traffic. Everyone in the city is out tonight. I came as fast as I could." Your excuse sounds bad even to you, but Robertson just nods.

"I realize I called you on short notice, Pete," he says, tamping down the tobacco with his thumb, "and I called you because I know you are usually dependable and also need the work. But you aren't established yet with Kate Cushing, and since she normally assigns the jobs . . ."

"I'm going to have to show up on time." You finish the sentence, looking at your shoes. The life of a free-lancer is not a whole lot of fun.

"Okay," Robbie says, lighting his pipe," Kate *and* Jonah *and* one of Jonah's free-lancers are in there. Look good for them, and there may be more assignments in the future. And tell Kate something came up—I'll be in my office if she needs me." With that, Robbie heads toward his office, leaving a cloud of pipe smoke behind him.

Turn to **101**.

97 "No dice, Kingpin," you say. "I'd sooner do a swan dive into Times Square than make a promise like that. If you want me to save *your* city, you'll just have to ante up the information."

The Kingpin of Crime sighs and returns to his desk. "I am sorry you feel that way, truly sorry," he says, depressing a button by his phone. "Since you refuse, I must use what us villains refer to as 'Plan B.' Your foe will take you and leave *my* world alone, so I will give you to him."

Behind you, there is the hydraulic hiss of panels sliding up into the ceiling. Wheeling, you see a small army of thugs issue from the opening. Glancing behind you, you see that the chair where Kingpin sat is now empty, and there is no sign of the crime lord. *How can someone that fat move that fast?*

The thugs approaching you through the open panel are armed with pipes, nets, and blackjacks. Do you wish to fight them (go to **112**), or try to escape (go to **40**)?

98 *I knew I saved up my webbing for something,* you think, forming the webbing into a shield.

Depending on how much juice he has in that thing, I've got a chance.

You walk into the doorway, web-spun shield in one hand, web-shooter ready in the other. You reach the doorway and you hear his voice, cracked by madness, shouting, "I have you now! Die, Spider, so I may be free!"

A huge bolt of energy, more powerful than you anticipated, hits your shield. The force of the blast rolls you back forty feet into the corridor.

You take 10 points of damage, and your shield is shredded. If your health is less than 0, you are unconscious, and your adventure ends here.

If you are only badly shaken, turn to **193**.

99

You make your leap, but the mugger was ready for any sudden moves and just scared enough to try something. You hear the ripping of cloth as you leap, and you feel a sharp pain in your side as the tip of the knife scratches you deeply. Reduce your Health by 3 points.

Blast, blast, BLAST! you think, reaching out to grab the wall some five feet above the attacker. *A moment slower and he would have skewered me. As it is, I'm going to have to see a good tailor.*

You grab the wall and turn to face your attacker. The symbol of your uniform peeks through your open shirt. The mugger may see it. He may just be aware of a man hanging by his fingertips to a vertical brick wall five feet above him. Either way, he's surprised, and it takes a moment before he tries to stab at you with his knife.

A moment is all you need. You deliver a savage kick to his jaw, a little harder than the situation merits. "First lesson of Mugging 101," you say to the mugger's prostrate form. "Never, EVER mug a guy in a funny outfit. It just makes him mad."

Realizing your words are falling on deaf ears, you clamber down the wall to make sure the mugger is still breathing. You hear someone coming, so it's up the side of the building again, this time making the full change into your Spider-Man outfit. By the time you are three stories up, you're in full uniform. Give yourself 1 point of Karma, then turn to **118**.

100 You look into the water and see your flashlight glowing dimly at the bottom of the sewer, slowly moving downstream, along with the alligator, dragged by the current. You almost consider going after it when you notice that there is another light source, a soft radiance from up the passage where the trail leads. *This may be a way out,* you think, *or a way in.* You proceed to **165** to follow the light.

101 "You wanted to see me?" you say, entering the conference room.

"No, I want to see Spider-Man's name under the column 'Recent Arrests'," snaps Jameson. "Where the blue thunder have you been?"

"Well, I—" you begin, trying to think of an explanation as you talk.

"I don't want to hear any excuses, Parker. A newspaper isn't built on excuses. It's built on dedication. Do you know what dedication is, Parker?"

"Well, I—"

"Dedication is what made this country great. Dedication is how I got where I am today. Dedication is showing up for meetings when I am supposed to. What do you think we are running here, Parker?"

"Well, I—"

"This is a newspaper, Parker, not some college social club where tardiness is noted by a green star by your name. A newspaper is a business, Parker. And in business, time is money. Millions are wasted each day on long coffee breaks and lunch hours, on people not showing up on time, wasting the time of others, yakking in halls. . . ."

You look around for support. Jameson's free-lancer looks at you and shrugs. He's apparently heard this routine before. Kate Cushing just stares at you in a steely glare that summarizes Jameson's ranting in a second. *You've failed me, Mr. Parker*, the glance says. *One more failure added to a long string of others. How long must we put up with you?*

After about five minutes of Jameson's speech, he seems to run out of steam, and Kate uses this moment to-break in and get the meeting rolling.

"Peter, this is Sam Karpierz." She motions to the other man in the room, who rises from his chair to shake your hand. He's a tall, rumpled man, a lean scarecrow whose clothes hang on him. His eyes, however, are alive and take you in in a single gaze.

"Sam works as a free-lancer for *NOW Maga-*

zine," she continues. "He's doing a series on fraud and thievery in the utilities. In his work, he's come up with an amazing fact. Sam?"

"Well," the scarecrow says as his blue eyes scan an open file folder. "There's a large amount of theft in most utilities—employees walking off with things, embezzlement and fraud in the upper ranks, organized criminal activity—the normal sort of thing. However, take a look at this." He shoves a clipping from a local suburban paper at you.

You read it aloud: " 'Dr. Clifford Jefferson, head of the South Brooklyn Psychiatric Facility, has been reported missing as of last Tuesday—"

"Other side, Parker!" snaps Jameson.

Sighing, you turn the clipping over, though your spider-sense begins a low buzzing. Make an Intuition FEAT. If the total is 12 or more, go to **114**; otherwise go to **17**.

102 As you swing, the Green Goblin reacts, faster than any normal human ever could. He catches your wrist in a grip that feels like iron. The expression on your opponent's face does not change, nor do his lips move as you hear him say, "Now, Spider-Man, you will perish with me!"

Robot! you realize, suddenly aware that the unexpected appearance of an old foe was just what the doctor ordered to throw you off guard long enough to let this happen. *The whole thing is a trap, and I fell for it! Wild and crazy, indeed!*

There is a high-pitched whine as the goblin glider climbs with its added load, then plunges down to meet the hard concrete of the Plaza below. You must get your hand loose or there will be Spider-Man all over the East Side!

Make a Strength FEAT roll. If the result is 11 or more, move on to **124**. Otherwise, go to **51**.

103

Your webs arch across the street, over the heads of the defenders, and into the mouth of the alleyway. One of the goons ditches his weapon when he sees the ball of webbing and flees down the alley. The other is not so quick, and is plastered against the stonework behind him.

One down, one to go, you think. Add 1 point to your Karma score *Now for Tweedledee's partner.* Launching yourself from the side of the building and into the alley's mouth, you pass over the heads of the Pegasus people. One of them shouts, "Watch it! He's got friends!"

"That's okay," you shout back, landing in the alley. "They can see him on visiting days!" Your escaping target is already halfway down the alley. If Tweedledummy had friends here, they're gone now. But where? Your spider-sense suddenly goes off full tilt. The goon is making for an open manhole, and he's running straight into danger!

"Watch out, you idiot!" you shout, already starting to leap ahead of the goon and stop him, when the alleyway suddenly heaves with a powerful explosion. The manhole blazes with fire, and you are knocked off your feet. Turn to **55**.

104 Thinking quickly, you brace the sagging rocks above you with both hands, and call to the workman who came down with you.

"Quick!" you shout, your voice carrying down the sewers. "Get me something to brace this wall with!"

The light that has been shining on your digging flickers and turns away, and you are left in the darkness for a moment. You hear the drip of water and the shouts of the workman to his fellow sewer workers. Your arms are beginning to tire, but if you let go, the entire street above could cave in.

After a short eternity, the light returns, with the workmen behind it. "Here you go, Spider-buddy," the spokesperson says, placing a large device next to you. "One handy-dandy sewer jack at your service." He turns a crank on one side of the tool and it expands against the ceiling, taking the weight off your aching shoulders. Add 1 point to your Karma score for holding up the ceiling.

"That was close," you say, and in that same instant, you notice the workman's light flashing down the passage that has been fully opened by the sudden shift. "That's funny," he says. "The sewer is supposed to end fifteen feet from here."

Instead, the sewer continues down into the darkness. Along the concrete floor of this unknown sewer, the algae and moss have been pushed aside, leaving a clear path into the depths of the city.

Proceed to **122**.

105 You and the others wander into the warehouse. Andrews holds both hands out, motioning at the emptiness.

Your own spider-sense is reacting dully, no more than a raspy itch in the back of your mind. *Something isn't right,* you think, noting the smooth floor. *It's like it's never been used!*

At that point you freeze in your tracks, not from any sudden insight but because your shoes have started to sink into the concrete!

You look down. Your penny loafers have definitely sunk into the concrete to the top of the soles, leaving nary a ripple. Your heels have also been swallowed. You wiggle your toes. It feels as if you are standing in your stocking feet on concrete.

You carefully lift one foot. It's like freeing yourself from a gooey muck, but your right shoe lifts out of the concrete, leaving the surface unmarred. You reach down to touch the surface, and it feels like a hard floor.

A normal person would be mystified by such a strange floor, but then, you are not a normal person. You've traveled between the stars and into other dimensions, and you've fought beings unknown to most of the world. You've battled alongside such world-class brains as Iron Man and Reed Richards. A little thing like a quicksand floor is not going to throw you.

You walk about ten feet, feeling as if you are walking through light snow, when you reach the edge of the strange area. The shoe-sucking zone seems to be about twenty feet wide at most, and it is located right in the center of the floor. Finally your shoes rest on the concrete. You draw out an empty film canister and, kneeling on the hard concrete, roll the the canister toward the area you came from. The canister rolls along the concrete until it reaches the edge of the affected area, then disappears into the floor. You touch that area. It's still hard as a rock.

A selective phasing? you wonder, tapping the concrete. The Vision can alter his molecular structure to pass through solid objects, and Shadowcat of the X-Men can phase her body out of sync with the atoms, but this is the first time you've seen such an otherwise inanimate substance that is selective. It apparently doesn't like living tissue, which is why your shoes stuck and you didn't.

"Find anything?" asks Sam, wandering up. Andrews is ordering his men around to check anything that looks like an exit, mostly around the perimeter of the warehouse. *They'd never notice this odd zone in the middle,* you think, *except by accident.*

"What's underneath here?" you ask.

"More concrete," answers the reporter. "About three feet of it. Then sewers, gas mains, the usual stuff, and a lot of bedrock. If you're thinking that crooks came up from below, forget it. I thought of that, but there'd have to be some sort of secret door. Whoever did this even took the dust, so if there was a door we'd see it."

"Look at this," you say, fishing out another roll of film and rolling it across the floor into the region where your shoes sunk.

The film canister rolls into the area and keeps on rolling, eventually coming to rest against the shoes of Andrews, the chief of security.

"Cute," says the chief, picking up the roll. "What next—marbles?"

"Uh . . . no thanks. How about a roller rink?" you suggest.

Andrews scowls at you. "Is there anything else?"

"I have a few more questions," says Sam.
"Can it wait until later?" the chief asks.
"I can hang around," Sam replies. "Peter, why don't you get those shots to the paper? I'll phone in the story later."
"Roger-dodger," you say, taking the roll back from Andrews sheepishly.
Whatever was responsible for that effect has turned it off somehow, you think. *Maybe it would be better if Spider-Man paid a visit to this place later.* Add 1 point to your Karma for discovering an important clue, then head for the door **(111)**.

106

"Do you know how much paperwork there is for an escaped criminal?" she asks, stooping to pick up the scattered papers.
"No, but if you hum a few bars, I'll try to pick it up," you say. She shoots you a glare that says, "Don't mess with me; it's been a bad day."
"What do you want now?" she asks, trying to reorganize the papers into some kind of order, then giving it up as a lost cause.
"How about if I get your runaway electric company back?" you say.
"Given a choice, I'd rather have a week in Jamaica, but it would make things easier," she says, picking up one official-looking form and quoting: 'If said incident involved super-powered

individuals, please designate on a separate form the nature, identities, and abilities displayed by said individuals and their bearing on the incident.' Can you imagine what it would be like if the Avengers had come by to help? At least they have this stuff on preprinted forms." She looks up at you. "Right. Information. What do you want?"

"Well," you say, "the last time we met, you were loudly handling the cleanup from that little kidnapping, so we didn't have too much time to chat. And I walked into the middle of the picture, so I have no real idea why you were there in the middle of Manhattan in the first place, unless it's standard procedure to ship dangerous criminals through the heart of the city in the early evening. So why don't you take it from the top, and tell me the whys and wherefores?"

Turn to **183**.

107 "There's your dust," you say, training your spider-beacon around the cavern-like sewers beneath the warehouse.

"Okay, I'll bite," says the security chief, who followed you down, "how did they do it?"

You flash your light against the ceiling. It is littered with small, red electrodes placed against the rock. "My best guess is that they set up some kind of specialized phasing field that allows certain materials through but not others. That way they could rob you blind without you noticing it, never enter the building, and take only what they wanted."

"Holy . . ." says Andrews, now more subdued. "So where did they take it?"

You shine the beam around a bit more. There is

a path through the sewer muck—a path about eight feet wide. Something has plowed the sewage up on either side of the path.

"Thataway, Kimosabi," you say. "I'm going on ahead. If I'm not back within an hour, call the police. And maybe the Avengers, while you're at it."

Andrews nods as he heads back for the surface. You step through the muck and follow the clear path of whatever carried the stolen wire away.

Proceed to **49**.

108

You sneak cautiously down the passageway and look into the room beyond, careful not to fully reveal yourself. A twisted machine looms in the center of the vault, sparks dancing off its metal sides as if it is alive. At its heart is Electro, trapped in a glass bubble and glowing like a star. At the top of the machine is Doctor Octopus, the mentally unbalanced master planner of the entire operation, waiting for you like a cat waiting by a mousehole. The barrel of the weapon is pointed at the door.

One thing for Doc Ock, he is never subtle, you think. *But what now? Into the ventilator* (move on to **138**)*? Dodge in closer* (go to **86**)*? Make myself a shield with webbing* (turn to **98** only if you still have webbing left to use).

Make your choice, hero, because Octopus awaits!

109

You land between the two goons, but they saw you coming. One is already turning to run; the other is bringing up his weapon to block your punch. You leap at the the one with the weapon, hoping to bowl him over and knock him into his fleeing companion.

In mid-leap, there is a blinding flash. You don't connect with the thug as the force of an explosion blasts you and the criminals out of the alleyway. As you are lifted bodily into the air, you have a brief glimpse of the alley and of an open manhole spitting fire like a small volcano. Go to **55**.

110 You approach the huge metal doors. *Something is rotten in the state of New York,* you think. *Huge metal doors. Hmmm . . .*

You dig out a spare metal cartridge of web-fluid and toss it at the doors. The intensity of the flash upon connection blinds you for a moment.

Makes sense, you think, *Electro, electrical supplies, huge metal doors. Put it all together and it spells T-R-A-P. Now, how to get through it without becoming a pile of spider-flavored bacon bits?*

You see the hovercraft and smile beneath your mask.

Go to **93**.

111 *Interlude.*

He sits alone, a spider in his web. If he thought of that phrase, he would not be amused, for amusement comes rarely to him in these days. His jaw is tight with rage; his eyes almost glow with the anger bottled inside him. He is a man obsessed, possessed with his hatred.

"Where IS he?" he snarls, he who considers himself the composer, no, the conductor of his own symphony of destruction. "He HAD to see the message. He MUST be on his way. I know he is out there waiting for me. I MUST have him brought to me."

On the computer console before him is a small statuette of Spider-Man, a penny-bank made years ago by some now-defunct toy company. An arm snakes out and grabs the statuette.

"I want him! I WANT HIM!" shouts the man, his voice rising and ringing in the room. "He will be brought to me and he will perish! THEN I will be free! Oh, yes, Doctor, only then will I be free!" The statuette shatters in his grip, sending a shower of plaster onto the computer keyboard.

Another man, dressed in dull green, enters while the master planner rants. The guard clears his voice softly, as if to remind his master that he is there.

"You? What now?" hisses the shadowy form.

"You wanted to know when Electro came to," says the guard. "He's ready again. And Rico and Luce have snatched that replacement wire you needed. They've got it set up now."

"Good," says the master, regaining his composure, drawing out the word as if it were a primitive curse. "Activate all the defenses. Keep the lines to our contacts open. Our foe will either come here directly or soon be delivered into our hands. Bring Dillon to the chambers."

The guard hesitates momentarily, and the master snarls, "GO! Leave this place with your fellow lackeys, and leave me to my triumph. But leave the Doctor. I want him to share my triumph!"

The guard vanishes into the darkness, and the madman at the center of his web croons over the shattered statuette of Spider-Man.

"Soon," he says. "Very, very soon."

End of Interlude. Turn to **137**.

112 There appear to be at least a dozen thugs, maybe more, closing in. The harsh light from the gooseneck lamp throws pitch-black shadows behind them, increasing their apparent numbers.

You reach back and pull the lamp off the desk and fling it at the first thug, a huge ape of a goon wielding a piece of pipe the size and shape of a rifle barrel. The lamp hits with a resounding thud, and

the lights go out in the room, save for a small square of city lights visible through the window.

You leap to the ceiling in the dark, as your foes collide in the area where you were before the lights went out. Clinging to the ceiling with your hands, you lash out with both legs, each knee catching a goon.

Your spider-sense is buzzing like a blue streak as a pair of arms surround one leg and pull. Your grip on the ceiling holds, but the ceiling does not. The ceiling panel gives way, and you are pulled into the mass of wildly swinging henchmen.

Your advantage lies in the fact that no matter who you hit, you are hitting a foe; that, and the fact that Kingpin has evidently ordered his pet trogs to bring in the merchandise alive, works to your advantage. All the same, you're taking an incredible beating from their lucky, well-placed punches.

Your spider-sense warns you of a blow aimed at your head, but you are restrained in your movement by the other battlers, and catch the blow on your shoulder. Sharp pains radiate down your arm.

It is a long fight. Your superior abilities are almost outweighed by their sheer numbers. Almost. When the smoke finally clears, you are standing in the wreckage of Kingpin's office, surrounded by unconscious thugs.

Take 15 points damage from all the blackjacks and other blunt instruments that have been used on you. If your Health is less than 0 as a result of this damage, your adventure is over. You may start again with your Karma score reduced by 1 point.

If you are well enough to go on, turn to **88**.

113 As you land on the machinery, sparks spread out from your fingers. You feel a tingle akin to your spider-sense, but otherwise the massive machine does you no damage. Atop it, the madman who has been trying for most of the evening to kill you is watching you, stock still.

OK, hero, now what? you wonder, as you see Doc Ock's arms begin to writhe along the sides of the machine. *Attack? Talk to him? Free Electro (who is still glowing and looks as if he is probably in pain)? Try to sabotage the machinery? He's had me on the run all evening, Now it's my turn. Think!*

If you want to free Electro, go to **18**. If you want to attack Doctor Octopus, turn to **201**. If you would prefer to talk to Octopus, proceed to **209**. If you want to break the machinery, go to **14**.

114 *South Brooklyn.* The name rings a bell. Of course! That's where they are holding Otto Octavius, better known as Doctor Octopus, for study and treatment. Can there be a connection? You make a mental note to follow that up later. Give yourself 1 Karma point for recognizing the name.

"Well, Peter?" says Cushing, uneasy with your silence.

"Oh, sorry," you say and begin to read the clipping aloud. Turn to **17**.

115

You wade into the stream, wondering if the flashlight is waterproof. The stream is not deep, coming just up to your chest at the midpoint, but it has an aroma that can be described only as pungent.

You are almost across when you see something moving toward you—a long, white shape that looks like a body floating in the water. Massive jaws open on the forward part of the white body, snapping as the creature approaches. You are about to share close quarters with a giant, New York City albino alligator!

You can try to run from the creature (move on to **90**), or fight the beast (go to **196**).

116

"Hold on," you say, putting your costumed foot in the door. The intern looks at you with bleary-eyed boredom. "You don't believe I'm Spider-Man, do you?"

"No. I just thought your mother dresses you funny." Another yawn. "Look, I'm missing roll call on 'Hill Street Blues,' so do you mind?"

"Not at all. Just watch this." You leap onto the side of the doorway and enter the room, walking on the ceiling.

"Um . . . er . . . ah . . . ohmigosh! You ARE Spider-Man!" The blond-haired man looks shocked, his eyes wide open now. "I mean, I'm sorry for the inconvenience and all, but, uh, why are you here? I mean, your presence could upset the patients. They're not on the firmest ground to start with, if you get my meaning."

The man's a swine, you think, but aloud you say, "My interest is purely professional. Is Otto Octavius still under observation here?"

"Doc Ock?" asks the intern, "Sure! He's still riding the disorient express, a member of our happy family. I'd let you see him, but he's been down in the dumps since Doc Jefferson disappeared, and I think that seeing you might just push him over the edge, at least in my medical opinion."

I liked him better when he was being offensive, you think. "Ock's doctor disappeared?" you say aloud.

"Into the night. Like Houdini. No one's seen him for a couple weeks now."

Interesting. "But Octavius is still here?"

"Still here. Not much on conversation, but he plays a mean game of chess," the intern says with a smile like an undertaker. "I wish I could show him to you. Really. Now can I go watch my show?"

You thank the intern and leave the facility. Give yourself 1 point of Karma for keeping your cool. *Ock is around, but his doctor is gone. Odd.* You think for a moment about another case involving the Green Goblin and his psychiatrist.

Harry Osborn, son of Norman Osborn, the original Green Goblin, sought psychiatric help. Harry's psychiatrist, envious of the power of the Green Goblin, used the information he gained from Harry to become the Green Goblin himself. That incarnation of the goblin later died, but there is a similarity between that case and this.

Is history repeating itself? you wonder. *Could Jefferson decide to take on the mantle of Doc Ock?* The very thought chills you.

You can check out Ock for yourself **(206)**, or try something else **(197)**.

117

About five minutes later, the Mayor pads into the kitchen. You have your mask pulled above your mouth and are nibbling on a Danish.

You pour the Mayor some coffee and offer him part of the Danish.

"Thanks," he says, sipping the black coffee. "I called around. The police have no warrants out on you, though I am tempted to issue one for disturbing a public official's sleep. Ditto for the federal government. I called Albany and woke the Governor, just to check."

"I don't think that Albany . . ." you begin.

"Neither do I," interrupts the Mayor, "but I have a few joys in my job. One of them is calling Albany and waking the Governor. If I don't sleep, he doesn't sleep.

"Finally," he continues, between bites of the Danish, "I started to think about it. If I were some kind of super-powered bozo, and I wanted someone to surrender, who would I call? I'd call the local TV stations."

He pauses for a moment, looking in his coffee cup. After a moment you prompt, "And . . ."

"The UN," he says.

"Pardon?" you ask.

"The UN," he repeats. "Whoever wants you for breakfast, and is mad enough to black out this fair city, wants you at the UN. So what are you waiting for?"

You set down the Danish, roll your mask back into place, and start to head for the door. "Thank you. I should have thought of that. I'm sorry to have troubled you about this . . ."

The Mayor waves your apology away. "I have some paperwork to do anyway. Just do me a favor. Two favors. One. Take care of the joker who is turning off the lights in my favorite city. Two. Next time, try the media first. If I ever want you to surrender, I'll tell them. Okay?"

"Yes, sir," you reply as you reach the door.

"One last thing," says the mayor. "There's a word. *Meshugga.* It means wildly crazy. Dangerously crazy. Whoever you are after may be that crazy. Be careful out there."

If the Mayor sighs as you leave, you don't notice it. Move on to **198**.

118 You reach the top of the ten-story building and see a city of ghosts spread out before you. Taxis and other cars cast cones of light straight ahead, creating rivers of light through blocks of darkness. It would be incorrect to say complete darkness, because private generators are providing minimal power to some buildings—weak lights like glow worms. The illusion is furthered by a number of weak lights in some windows. Candles?

To the north, you see a beacon of light. The Fantastic Four would have their own power supply in order to maintain all their machinery and experiments. *I wonder how many New Yorkers will blame them for this power outage. Or blame me!* You think of a particular publisher with a toothbrush mustache and make a wish that he is currently trapped in an elevator. Between floors. Without his cigars.

Looking east, you're surprised to see lights in Queens and Brooklyn, a fairy-tale dotting of lights from private homes, pierced by lights from occasional factories. There's a squealing whine overhead as a jet passes too low over the city. Kennedy International and LaGuardia must be having fits. Even if they have power, the big black spot that is normally a sea of lights from the heavily populated borough must be creating all sorts of havoc.

Okay, hero, so what now? you think. *How do you track down a blackout? Look for a master switch set in the off position, with Doctor Doom gloating over it? Where would all that energy go?*

There's a flash as lightning arches up from the East River, and you get your answer. Turn to **89**.

119

You can press on to the warehouse, or you can retreat and try something else. If you want to press on, go to **158**. If you want to try something else, go to **137** and make another choice.

120

Discretion is the better part of valor, you think, and turn on your heels to run. The sight of five former foes at once has rattled you. *Maybe it would be better to come back with reinforcements. Yeah!*

That's the ticket! Get the Fantastic Four or the Avengers or someone.

Your thoughts are racing, and you can hear your pursuers. You look back to see their shadows moving toward you down the passage.

You are so wrapped up in the nerve-racking role of being the pursued that you fail to notice a thin wire net that has been dropped over the opening to the complex. As you plow into the net, a powerful electrical charge shoots through you. With one last surge of strength you snap the net and stagger into the stream beyond. Your unconscious body is found on the shores of Jersey the next day.

Your adventure is over. You may try again, using the knowledge you have gained from this adventure, but subtract 3 points from your initial Karma (for running away from a fight).

121 The darkness of the alley is brilliantly lit for half a heartbeat. The ground heaves, and cracks run through the walls. You are thrown clear of the mouth of the alley and only avoid injury from a piece of flying pipe by curling into a rolling crouch.

You land on the overturned security truck. Smoke drifts through the alleyway. Your two playmates are sprawled at the mouth of the alley. Guards from the Pegasus Project are already checking them, while others are moving down the alley itself. A tall blond woman dressed in a blue jumpsuit stands in the midst of the scene, barking orders. Her hair is pulled back into a tight bun, and she seems to be taking the entire situation, explosion included, as a personal affront.

"Get down the alley!" she shouts at a pair of guards. "Try to find them!"

"Find who?" you ask, jumping down next to her. She glances at you long enough to know that you are still among the living, but doesn't reply. *Find who?* You still want to know. You thought you already took care of the crooks who were involved.

One of the guards approaches you and the blond woman. "I've gotten in touch with the New York Police Department. The paramedics are on the way. The police have put out an All Points Bulletin for them."

"All Points Bulletin? Who are you looking for?" you ask, but again you receive no answer. "I just saw two goons. How many more were there?"

Another of the guards comes back from the alley. "Explosion in the sewers, ma'am. Awful mess. Must've been an arms depot or something. No sign of them. They must have had a vehicle waiting on the other side of the alley."

"Now, wait just a cockamamie minute!" you shout, twisting around to face the head honcho. "WHO is missing? WHO got away? And WHO are you looking for?"

She stares at you for a moment, as if you just wandered onto the scene. "I suppose you would need to know," she says. "You missed seeing them take him away."

"Let's say that, given the fact that I almost had my head handed to me by thugs with blasters and bombs, I'm more than mildly curious." Mentally you are counting to ten.

"We were escorting a prisoner from Project Pegasus to a parole hearing when we were ambushed," she replies. "The prisoner's name was Maxwell Dillon. You probably know him better as Electro."

Go to **69**.

122 "Come into my parlor, said the spider to fly," you say quietly, thinking, *Or is it, "said the Electro to the Spider?"*

You dig out your spider-beacon from your belt, but the workman who has been helping hands you his flashlight.

"That little-bitty light isn't going to help you if you're going that direction," he says. "Take this one. Its halogen beam will light up a hundred yards down here. It's also shockproof, which means you can use it on the crocagators."

You take the flashlight, saying, "Thanks . . . er . . ."

"Ed. Just call me Ed," says the worker, giving a lopsided grin.

A sewer worker named Ed. Only in New York, you think. You tell Ed and his buddies that if they don't hear from you in two hours, they should go to the police with what they know. With that, you head down the path.

Off to see the Wizard. Or the Doctor. Or whoever, you think, reaching a bend that will carry you out of sight of the repairmen. You turn back, wave, and you are gone.

Turn to **49**.

123

Changing into your civilian clothes, you cross to the door and ring the bell. A blond-haired intern in a loud Hawaiian shirt opens the door and peers at you through sleepy eyes.

"Uh-huh?" he says, yawning.

"Excuse me for calling at such a late hour," you say, smiling as broadly as you can. "My name is Peter Parker. I'm from the *Daily Bugle*, and I'm interested in one of your patients here."

"Uh-huh." He yawns again. "Look, visiting hours are tomorrow at nine o'clock. Dr. Jefferson is still missing. Franco is still dead. All's right with the world. Good night." He starts to close the door.

You shove a foot in the door before he can close it all the way. "Excuse me. What did you say about Dr. Jefferson?"

"Aren't you here about our great missing head-shrinker, specialist in the id and ego of classic crack-ups like Doc Ock?"

"Uh, no." You shake your head. "I was kind of interested in Dr. Octavius himself. You see, my aunt and he were engaged for a while, and she worries about him, so I promised—"

"To look in on the little maniac," he finishes your sentence. Another sigh. "Parker, huh? I think Ock mentioned your aunt once when Dr. Jefferson let me sit in on one of his sessions. Well, tell your aunt that Otto Octavius is resting as well as can be expected for a man who is afraid of spiders and whose analyst has disappeared, okay?"

"Hang on!" Your foot goes in the closing door again. "You say his analyst has actually disappeared?"

"Read my lips. Gone. Evaporated. Vamoosed. Scrammed. Took the last train to Clarksville. It was in the papers. One day here, next day gone. Nobody knows where. Now, if you don't let me close this door, I'm going to take off your leg. I'm missing the opening credits of 'Hill Street Blues.' "

You step back and the door shuts in your face. *Ock is here, but his doctor is gone. Curious. I wonder if that pale-faced intern is right about Ock resting comfortably.* Give yourself 1 point of Karma for because you got the information you wanted peacefully.

You can change into Spider-Man and check out the windows **(206)**, or take the young man at his word and try something else **(197)**.

124 You wrench yourself free at the very last moment, every tendon straining to put enough distance in your leap to clear the range of the blast.

You land less than gracefully on one shoulder, taking 1 point of damage to your Health. Then you are knocked back further by the blast of the pseudo-Goblin and *his* glider plunging into the center of the UN Plaza's courtyard. The concrete heaves and the trees shudder with the force of the blow.

You stand and rotate the arm you landed on. *Painful, but no major damage. Lucky, considering what would have happened had I been riding that thing when it plowed into the ground.* You walk up to inspect the wreckage.

Move on to **58**.

125

Taunting the publisher of a major daily paper is cruel and vicious. It is also fun when the publisher in question is J. Jonah Jameson.

You peer through the window. Robertson has left the room, but Cushing, Jameson, and a third lanky man you don't recognize are there. Cushing and the lanky gentleman are seated at the conference table. Jameson is pacing nervously.

"You know," says Cushing, looking at the pacing Jameson over the top of her glasses, "Robertson called Parker first, but we could easily assign another photographer, maybe roust one of the staff to meet Sam at the Battery. Parker shows talent from time to time, but his career is almost entirely built on his pictures of Spider-Man."

"Someone drop my name?" you ask, swinging into the office.

"That maniac wall-crawler!" shouts Jameson. "What are you doing here?"

"I was just passing by when I saw an open window, heard my name mentioned, and thought, 'Gee, its been a long time since I've had a heart-to-heart chat with my old buddy Jameson.' " You throw an arm around the publisher affectionately before he can dodge out of the way. "Did I tell you kids that Jonah saved my life at Anzio? Jumped on a grenade to save my platoon. Of course, it really was a rotten apple, but it's the thought that counts. A penny for yours, Jonah?"

"Look here, you costumed idiot!" sputters Jameson, but you notice that Cushing and the other man are hiding smiles at the publisher's discomfort. "You are interrupting a private meeting, not to mention trespassing! GET OUT OF HERE THIS INSTANT!" Jameson makes his point by slamming both fists on the table.

"Well, if you're going to be that way about it, you have to say the magic word," you reply.

"MAGIC WORD?" bellows the publisher.

"Please."

Jameson's face turns crimson with rage.

"Well . . ." you say with a smirk, "since you put it so nicely, how can I refuse? Oh, one more thing," you say, turning from the window and wondering if Jameson is going to have cardiac arrest now or later. "I ran into a harried free-lance photographer who got caught in traffic. He says to tell Robbie he'll be a little late, but he's en route. Ta-ta, troopies! And, Jonah, better cut down on those cigars. Looks like they give you high blood pressure."

Jameson's response is as loud as it is unprintable. You dive out the window and adhere to the wall outside, quickly scrabbling over to the window in case jolly Jonah leans out of the office to hurl a few more invectives at you. Teasing Jameson is cruel, of course (reduce your Karma by 1), but it sure is fun.

Turn to **96**.

126 You are over the fence and among the warehouse buildings before you begin to question the wisdom of your actions. *This is, after all, a matter of trespassing.* Reduce your Karma by 1 point as you continue on, sticking to the shadows as much as possible.

Make an Intuition FEAT roll. If the result is 16 or more, go to **158**. If the result is 12, 13, 14 or 15, go to **60**. If the result is less than 12, go to **170**.

127 The mugger is easy to find, even given that the only steady source of light is the passing traffic. Your prey keeps looking back to see if you're following him. Convinced that you are, he dodges out into the street. There's a blare of horns, and an off-duty cab stops inches in front of him. Startled, the mugger drops your wallet and the rest of your items and, dashing to safety on the far side of the street, slams into a crowd of milling New Yorkers.

You stop and pick up your things, then look up to see if the thief is still in sight. His luck seems to be worse than yours, as one of the people he slammed into was one of New York's Finest. A cop. One that looks like he's dealt with the mugger before, given the way he is holding him. That's one mugger that's not doing any more business for the duration of this disaster.

You smile and, slipping back into the alley, finish changing into Spider-Man. You are out of the alley and up the side of the building before anyone else happens by. Go to **118**.

128

You hit the Green Goblin with strands of webbing fired from both of your wrists. One strand adheres to the Goblin's goblin glider, while the other smacks the foe straight in the eyes.

Not waiting to see if this Green Goblin somehow has the ability to fly while blinded, you rush directly beneath the oncoming glider and keep on running, hoping to pull the weblines taut and flip both machine and rider.

It works better than you had hoped. The Green Goblin, intent on rushing your last position, guns his turbine up to full speed, such that when you pull the strands taut, both rider and machine plunge head-first into the concrete at full tilt. A fire ball illuminates the evening sky and the blast cracks several of the glass panes of the UN's main gallery.

Ohmigosh, you think, rushing up to the place where the glider went down. *I just wanted to stop him, not kill him.* Then you notice that there is no body in the wreckage, only a mass of circuitry and burning metal. Your foe was little more than a killing machine. Move on to **58**.

129 Your feet pad across the concrete, and you notice the area is lit, though not well lit. A single light every twenty feet shines dimly, giving the impression of a coal mine.

Suddenly the passageway widens into a larger, dark room. You see nothing and hear only an electronic clicking and buzzing. Your spider-sense is also buzzing, and you are reaching for your spider-beacon when the lights come on and you see that you are surrounded!

Go to **77**.

130 You agree to go with Reed on his investigation of the strange object in orbit. A short trip to the Fantastic Four's launch site later, the team's rocket is lifted into a near-earth orbit.

The UFO turns out to be an emissary of the Ovoid race, monitoring Earth transmissions to determine if the civilization is advanced enough to merit working out a trade agreement. The Ovoids themselves are tall, thin, hairless, and have yellowish skin. They have extraordinary mental powers, in particular telekinesis, and have a highly advanced civilization.

While impressed with the local technology and in particular your own ability to walk on walls, the Ovoids are concerned that the rival nation-states would make negotiation too difficult and decide to wait until Earth has a unified government. You and Richards are invited to a wonderful dinner with the Ovoid trade delegation, and you impress your hosts with your knowledge of old TV space shows.

However, the Ovoids have nothing to do with the blackout of New York City. They had assumed it was some quaint cultural festival. By the time you and Reed return to Earth, the entire situation involving the blackout has been resolved by other super-powered individuals in your absence. The *Bugle* carries an editorial saying, in effect, that when the city was endangered, the so-called hero Spider-Man ran like a coward and hid until the danger was over.

Your adventure is over. You may start again, using what you have learned so far, but you must reduce your starting Karma total by 2 to reflect this additional knowledge.

131

You decide that discretion is the better part of valor and carefully empty your pockets onto the pavement. Handkerchief. Wallet. Keys. A couple rolls of film.

"Good move," says your assailant, knocking you across the back of the head with the handle of the knife, "A pleasure doing business with you."

You're dazed for just a moment, but in that time the mugger has scooped up your wallet and keys and headed for the street.

Do you want to follow him **(171)** or let him go so you can change into Spider-Man **(57)**?

132

One strand of webbing is stopped by the electrical force of the Green Goblin's shock bolts, while the other strikes home, hitting the Green Goblin square in the face.

Let's see you drive that buggy with web-glop all over your evil eyes, you think. But that is exactly what the Goblin does. The turbine of his glider rises. He banks and then dives straight at you.

Make an Agility FEAT roll to dodge out of the way. If the result is 13 or less, go to **28**. If the result is 14 or more, move on to **147**.

133 The room erupts with fire and smoke as the figure of Doctor Octopus on the bed explodes in a mass of flame and twisted metal. You throw yourself out the window to avoid most of the blast.

Make an Endurance FEAT roll. If the total is 14 or more, turn to **168**. If it is less than 14, go to **173**.

134 You lie there for what seems like the longest time, fighting for each breath against the ton of debris on top of you. It feels as if an elephant has sat on you in spite. *Or Kingpin*, you think, conjuring the image of the corpulent Kingpin of Crime, master of the underworld, sitting on an opponent. You laugh, but that makes the pains in your chest all the worse.

You are about to give up and let the darkness take you, when you see lights and hear voices. Hands grab at you and drag you out of the fallen area.

Your friend with the light escaped and has brought the other workers to where you are buried. It takes a while, but they free you from the debris. You inhale the "fresh" air and feel a sharp pain in your side. *Probably cracked a rib*, you think ruefully.

You suffer 10 points of damage from the collapse. If your Health is currently 0 or less, your adventure is over, as you are in no shape to continue. You may start again, with your Karma reduced by 1 point. If you are able to continue, turn to **84**.

135

The noise starts with the blaring of horns. With every traffic light in the city out of order, every intersection becomes an impenetrable snarl. The horns start blaring, echoing off the sides of the cold, dark buildings.

Then come the people, the shout of voices, the trample of a thousand footsteps. Out of the subways and the buildings, the now-dark theaters and stores, anyone who can reach street level does so. A common human thought—in the dark, look for light—is written over the entire population of the city. But the whole city is dark; the entire population is in a dark closet, with no way out.

The crush of people on the street increases. A throng of people push you and Sam Karpierz against a wall. There is a rising sense of panic in the air. Is this a job for Spider-Man?

If you wish to get away from Sam and change into Spider-Man, go to **66**. If you want to stay in your Peter Parker identity and stick with Sam, turn to **139**.

136 You bound out of the chamber just as the machine starts to smoke and the ceiling caves in. The walls and floor are buckling as you run at top speed out of the complex, only stopping to grab Doctor Jefferson, the imprisoned psychiatrist, and head out. Behind you is the sound of explosions.

From the sewer you make your way to the surface. There is one last explosion, this one reaching the surface (an abandoned garbage dump) and spreading light (and garbage) into the sky.

"You think they . . ." the doctor starts to ask, his voice faltering.

"Survived?" you say, "Don't know. Their kind has a way of turning up. For now, one more bad-guy plan has gone smash, leaving us to pick up the pieces." The pair of you watch the fire and listen for the approaching sirens as the police come to investigate. You have saved the city, and your adventure is over.

137 You sit there, perched on the top of a twenty-story skyscraper, looking north at the city. No one would know by looking that just a few hours ago this island metropolis was plunged into blackness by some madman, a madman who could likely do it again. A madman with a colossal grudge against you, Spider-Man.

The question is, which madman? You've made more enemies in your career than most, some of them incredibly powerful. Doc Ock, Hobgoblin, Doomsie, the Frightful Four, Vulture—the list goes on and on, a fact that is not the least bit reassuring. Electro is on the loose as well, but Electro has rarely used underlings. He usually teams up

with another super-powered felon when he isn't operating alone.

Somehow, though, everything ties in together: the springing of Electro, the power blackout, the thefts of electrical equipment, the writing in the sky. . . . It all adds up to one thing: someone doesn't like you.

Well, you think, *I can sit on my brains and worry, or I can go out and try to get to the bottom of this. I think getting to the bottom is the better choice of the two, but where do I start?*

You have a number of choices available to you. You may make each of the following choices only once. Mark off each choice you make with a pencil, so you don't choose the same path again. The choice you make may eventually refer you back to this entry, which will allow you to make another choice. Your choices are:

1) Check out the location of criminals with the same MO (*modus operandi*, or method of

working) as you have observed. That is, find out where all the villains who have some relation to electricity are. Go to **10**.

2) Check with Captain Nash, the leader of the Pegasus forces in the fight with Electro's kidnappers. If Captain Nash and her group were heading for the federal lock-up, there's a chance she's still there. Turn to **156**.
3) Investigate warehouse #12 in the Battery Con Ed storage area. Go to **164**.
4) Check out the scene of Electro's break-out again. Turn to **163**.
5) Contact the Kingpin of Crime. This powerful, evil man is aware of all that transpires in the underworld of this city. He may be able to tell you who is responsible. Turn to **53**.
6) Surrender. Find out who wants you so badly by walking directly into the lion's mouth. Then hit your would-be captor when he's not looking. Go to **175**.
7) Give up. If someone that powerful wants Spider-Man out of action, maybe it would be better for Spider-Man to cease to be. Go to **185**.

138

Trusting that Jefferson is correct and the vents are not monitored, you rip out the grillwork and crawl into the air ducts. After about five minutes you reach another grill. Looking out, you see an incredible sight.

It could best be described as an electrical elephant. It is a huge, almost obscene machine, occupying most of the room. At its core is Electro, glowing like a star and apparently in pain. At its crown, riding the elephant, is Doctor Octopus, awaiting your appearance at the doorway. The "trunk" of the elephant, the barrel of the weapon, which is probably what did the skywriting, is pointed at the doorway.

Definitely the work of a disturbed mind, you think, as you look at your foe while working the grillwork off the vent. *At least I am out of the line of fire.*

"Where is he . . . ?" hisses the doctor, his mechanical arms adjusting power levels and turning dials on the huge machine. "Why hasn't he appeared?"

"Sorry, Ock!" you shout, leaping from your hiding place. "Had to use the servant's entrance."

You leap out onto the machinery, where the beam cannot hit you, and go to **113**.

139

"Any suggestions?" you shout at Sam as the noise of the milling crowd rises to the verge of panic. In the distance, you hear the breaking of glass.

Karpierz shakes his head and points back to the door of the *Daily Bugle* building. You nod and force your way back into the lobby, leading the way. It's like swimming upstream, and were it not for your enhanced strength, both you and Karpierz would be swept away with the rest of the masses.

You find a relatively quiet corner and sit down in the lobby. Already the security guard has dug out his flashlight and candles, casting the first floor in an eerie glow.

"This may take a while," says Karpierz, "especially if there's a cascade effect."

"Cascade effect?" you ask, digging out your

camera and loading it with film.

"Right," replies the writer. "A power overload blows one safety device, which shuts down part of the system it monitors. The power that system would carry is then channeled into other systems that are already overloaded, causing their safety devices to shut them down, with the power going to other systems, and so on. Which means that one blowout can wreak havoc with the entire eastern seaboard."

"Sort of like dominos?" you ask.

"Right"—Sam's scarecrow head nods—"except that one domino knocks down two, which knock down four, which knock down eight."

"So what's our next move?"

"Wait it out," replies Sam. "Anyone who is connected with Con Ed is going to be humming tonight and not have time for interviews. In the meantime, you might as well get shots of the people milling on the street. Here." He scribbles something down on his business card. "If we get separated, this is where we'll meet."

The pair of you make your way back outside.

Turn to **202**.

140 A quick survey of the Plaza reveals nothing of import beyond the wreckage of the "Goblin" and his glider. The sirens are getting louder and, given what has just happened here, it may be best if you talk to the police at a later date—like invite them over for next Thanksgiving dinner.

Climbing the side of the UN building, you fire a webline across the street and swing off just as the first police arrive to investigate. If someone saw you, no mention was made. If anything, the next day's paper will carry something about terrorism.

Return to **137**.

141

You stick by Sam as everyone converges on Number 12, just two down from the suspect warehouse 14 from which the supplies have been disappearing. There are about a dozen security people in the storage complex, and they have all the ground-level exits covered by the time you arrive.

Andrews bellows orders at the top of his lungs until the alarm is cut off. You take a few shots of security people running about. Sam takes notes. Someone brings Andrews a bullhorn as the siren finally dies.

"Attention in there!" shouts the chief of security, his amplified voice echoing through the area. "You are trespassing on property belonging to a private corporation and are hereby ordered to present yourselves at the main doors with your hands up. Do you understand?"

Silence reigns inside the building.

After half a minute, Andrews uses the bullhorn again. "You have two minutes to give yourselves up, or officers will come in after you. I repeat, you have two minutes."

Still silence. A minute crawls by, then the second. The guards eye each other nervously. No one knows what is inside the warehouse.

"Okay," sighs Andrews, motioning to one of his men. "Open the doors, but be careful."

One guard pulls back the latch and slides the warehouse door open. It rasps slightly on its well-worn runners, and the noise sounds like an opening tomb.

Andrews is in first, his gun drawn. A couple more security men are behind him, then you and Sam Karpierz. You are stopped by what you see.

The warehouse is brightly lit by emergency lights designed to banish shadows from every nook and cranny. No one should be able to hide among the supplies.

But there are no supplies. The warehouse is completely empty.

Turn to **73**.

142 Your lunge from the water is not fast enough. The white alligator grabs you by a leg, and the two of you tumble into the water.

You drop the flashlight and slam the creature on the nose with your fist. It lets go of its grip, and you drag yourself up on the far shore. Not following, the white gator continues his swim downstream through the darkness.

Take 10 points of damage from the alligator's bite. If your Health is 0 or less as a result of the damage, your adventure is over. Your unconscious form is discovered the next day.

If you are still among the conscious, turn to **23**.

143

The figure on the turbine-powered goblin glider passes between the empty flagpoles of the UN and banks toward you for another attack.

Before he can let loose another blast of his super-powered electro-gloves, you are ready with a double blast of webbing.

Make an Agility with Webbing FEAT roll. If you roll 18 or less, turn to **25**. If you roll a 19, 20, or 21, go to **132**. If you roll a 22 or more, proceed to **128**.

144

You hear a satisfying "Oomph," and the pressure of the knife on your back is removed. Turning around, you see the shadowy form of the mugger. Give yourself 1 point of Karma as you change into your costume, then go to **118**.

145

You stand for a moment, looking at the shattered remains of Mysterio. *Robot,* you realize, *and wired to shock on contact. How many of the others as well?*

The others are moving toward you. Picking yourself up, you run to the far exit, where there is a switch and a metal door. Do you pull the switch (go to **153**), or try the door (turn to **47**).

146

The shots are coming from nearby. Swinging around the corner, you get the full picture from three stories above street level.

The center of the street is blocked by an overturned armored security truck. The truck bears the insignia of a blue horse's-head, but otherwise looks like U.S. Government standard issue. The truck's massive rear door has been blown off its hinges and is lying nearby. Army Jeeps, also with the horse's head symbol, are pulled over in front and back of the truck—apparently escorts for whatever was inside.

The occupants of the Jeeps, men and women dressed in blue uniforms, have piled out and are using the vehicles for cover. Their attackers are across the street, crouched in an alleyway: two men, dressed in green bodysuits, carrying huge weapons that look like World War II bazookas. These weapons are the source of the unearthly crackling you heard earlier, and the pair are firing random bolts of yellowish lightning at the guards

in the Jeeps, keeping them pinned down.

The smoke from the fight clears for a moment and you see, in neat lettering beneath the symbol on the truck, the word "Pegasus." *Good gravy!* you suddenly realize. *The boys and girls in blue are from Project Pegasus!*

Pegasus is an energy project located in upstate New York, funded by the Department of Energy. In the past, the project has investigated alternate forms of energy, including those possessed by super-powered bad guys, a number of whom are your old foes. An empty armored truck does not bode well. *At least I know whose team I'm on. Whoever would try to knock over a Pegasus transport has to be up to no good.*

You're not sure why these two groups chose a New York street to fight in, but it's apparent that the guys in green are not too worried about inflicting civilian casualties. This looks like a job tailor-made for the web-spinning wonder, and it might be a good time to pick up a few bucks shooting Spider-Man in action. Should you wade into battle, or should you take the time to set up your camera first?

If you set up the camera, go to **76**. If you leap into combat, go to **87**.

147

You run at full tilt to get out of the way of the oncoming glider, and at the last moment throw yourself behind a low concrete pedestal. Protected in your hiding place, you are unaffected by the blast that shakes the entire courtyard.

Looking up, you see a sight that could have come out of World War II. The wreckage looks like a crashed plane brought down by enemy fire.

Walking up, you notice something else. No body. Or rather, the "body" of the Green Goblin is nothing more than part of the glider—a robot.

Move on to **58**.

148 You look straight at Vulture as you leap toward him. You are more than ready for a good fight. Go to **208**.

149 You and Sam dash out into the night. Security men are already hustling across the field toward the sound of the alarm. "Warehouse 12!" bellows Andrews.

The sound pierces the night air and makes talk difficult. You motion to Sam to head one direction around to the building and indicate that you'll circle around the other way. He nods and heads off. Instead of heading to where you indicated, you go in the opposite direction from the confusion, looking for a shadowy spot in which to change into your costumed alter ego.

In a matter of mere moments, you have slipped into something more comfortable and are moving along the walls and roofs toward the warehouse. The warehouse is alive with lights and activity, and about a dozen security people have ringed the building. The alarm has been disconnected.

You want to see what's going on inside that warehouse, and it looks like rooftop access is as good a way as any. Besides, with the forces of justice converging from all sides, the crooks will have to get out somehow, and they may have jet-packs.

Make an Agility FEAT to see if you can manage to reach the rooftop undetected. Roll one die and add the result to your Agility score. If the total is 14 or more, turn to **27**. If it's less than 14, go to **188**.

150

Choosing your way carefully, you pick a path through the slippery goo and reach the other side. At that moment, you think you see movement in the water: probably another rat or something. Ahead there is a light other than your own. Dimming your flashlight, you check out the light at the end of the tunnel.

With my luck it'll be an oncoming train, you think. Proceed to **165**.

151

Not the easiest shot in the world, you note, *but if I aim it just right, I can catch the pair of them. Like so!* You press the hidden plates beneath your gloves, squirting two arching streams of web-fluid over the heads of the surprised Project Pegasus guards and into the alleyway.

Make a FEAT roll using your Agility with Webbing skill. If the total is 18 or less, go to **50**. If the total is 19, 20, or 21, turn to **103**. If it's 22 or more, go to **41**. Remember to add any Karma you wish to spend before you make the roll.

152 You turn on your spider-beacon and crawl into the pipe. It goes into the hillside beneath street level for about fifty feet before opening into a large section of the New York sewer system.

Your light falls on something silvery in the muck. Carefully digging it out, you find that it is a heavy, foot-long flashlight. Its beam is still fresh, indicating it was dropped here recently.

By accident or design? you wonder, turning off your spider-beacon and flashing the more powerful light around the sewer. To the right, the slime and muck have been pushed up, as if a bulldozer has passed through this part of the sewers.

That's an invitation if I ever saw one, you think. *Follow the slimy green road. I wonder what kind of wizard lives at the other end?*

Watching your footing very carefully, you start down the trail into the depths beneath the city.

Move on to **49**.

153 You pull the switch down, and the low-level clicking and buzzing of machinery in the room fades. You look back at your foes, and they are frozen in position.

Dumb robots, you think. *I knew the Sinister Six couldn't have staged a reunion bash, even to bash Spidey.* These little playmates were obviously guards for the main gates, and the switch allows someone from this end to shut them down so personnel can go in and out. *Simple once you know it. Pull the plug and they all wind down.*

The metal door hums and rises into the ceiling. *Five down, and it's obvious who the sixth is,* you think, passing on into the next corridor. Proceed to **169**.

154

You lunge out of the glare of the spotlights, making bounding handsprings across the wall. Some of the guards are trigger-happy, and a staccato burst of gunfire erupts from below. None of the bullets find a living target, but they splatter against the bricks of the warehouse wall, sending small chips everywhere.

Make an Agility FEAT roll. A total of 13 or less indicates that you've taken 3 points of damage from shards of flying brick. If your total is 14 or more, you escape the deadly glare of the spotlight, but you must reduce your Karma score by 1 point for getting yourself into such a sticky situation in the first place.

Now is not the best of times for a friendly neighborhood webspinner, you think, ducking back to where you stored your civilian duds. *Perhaps Peter Parker will do better where Spider-Man is unwelcome.*

Turn to **15**.

155

The "spokesman" flashes his light around the wreckage left underground by the blast. There is a thick smell of something smoldering, and the workman shouts to be heard over the steady din of water running over shattered concrete.

"The main part of the blast was this way," says the workman, making his point by panning the light over a mess of shattered concrete that almost fills the passageway. "The other way"—he flashes the light to the area behind you—"is almost as bad, and it leads to a dead end, according to the plans."

"Such an option," you say as you glance forward and back at the equally dismal-looking stretches of alleyway. Which way do you choose to go?

If you wish to go forward toward the main line of the sewer, turn to **72**. If you prefer to go the way that leads to a dead end, go to **79**. If you want to give up, leave the sewer, and try something else, return to **10**.

156 Capt. Patricia Amber Nash, commander of the Pegasus security team assigned to delivering Electro to his parole hearing, sits alone in an office in the Justice Building. In front of her are reams of paper. She is carefully ignoring the papers and staring at the ceiling, leaning her chair back on its hind legs. She might be lost in thought or just daydreaming.

Hanging upside down, you tap on the window. The sudden noise catches her by surprise, and it is only by grabbing the table that she avoids pitching backward to the floor. As it is, she scatters papers throughout the office.

Rising from the table, she stomps over to the window you are hanging outside of with as much decorum as she can muster. Through the insulated glass, she mouths the words "What the heck do you want?" She doesn't look pleased.

"Dinner and a movie?" you shout back, loud enough to be heard through the glass. "But I'll

settle for some information. How about letting me in before someone sees me out here and calls the cops?"

She looks at you for a long moment, as if weighing the options. Then she unlatches the pane and opens it. "Come in, then," she says, "and make it quick. It's getting cool out there." Turn to **106**.

157

The lights come on at Gracie Mansion after you've been banging on the door for fifteen minutes. You are expecting some minor level secretary to answer the door, so you are surprised by the distinguished balding gentleman who opens the door, dressed in a bathrobe and slippers.

"How'm I doing?" says the sleepy figure, yawning. "And what time is it?"

"Sorry to bother you so late, Mr. Mayor," you

say as he motions you into the foyer, "but I'm here to surrender."

The mayor fishes a set of reading glasses out of his robe pocket and, placing them on his nose, looks over the tops at you in disbelief. "Surrender?"

"Yes, sir," you say, "there was a blackout and these fiery letters demanding that I surrender." You look as innocent as anyone can who is wearing a mask. "The note was less than specific about whom I was to surrender TO."

"So you thought you'd start out by surrendering to me and work your way down." The mayor chuckles. "Look, son, the kitchen is through those doors. There are some Danish rolls in the bread box, and I'll put the coffee on. I'll make some phone calls and be right in." Proceed to **117**.

158 You slip onto the roof without further incident and in through a skylight.

No way the thieves could have removed the wire coils through that little skylight, or through the walls, you note, landing on the smooth concrete floor. *Only one way to go then: down.*

Bunching your hands together, you make a mighty swing at the floor. Make a Strength FEAT roll. If the result is 12 or more, go to **75**. If it is less than 12, go to **65**.

159 "You know your timing stinks," says Security Chief Andrews, slamming another file folder of forms down on his desk. Behind him, the glass vibrates with the low whine of generators.

"We had an appointment," replies Sam calmly.

"Right," huffs the chief, "and you thought that a little thing like a power blackout in Manhattan wouldn't require any work at all and I could talk to you in my wealth of free time, eh?"

"Was the blackout confined to Manhattan alone?" you ask, knowing the answer.

"Uh-huh," grunts Andrew, opening the file folder and staring at the top report in the apparent hope that you and Sam will fade into the woodwork. A moment passes, and you fail to do so. Looking up, Andrews continues, "You see, that's what makes it kind of strange. A blackout of that size should have blacked out the entire eastern seaboard. It's called—"

"A cascade effect," you finish, "where failure of one part of the system causes other parts to fail."

"Uh, right," says Andrews. "Anyway, the stuff I've got here"—he pats the stack of papers—"indicates the juice was turned on coming into the city, but it got sidetracked after it came in, as if someone plugged into the system and took the power."

"Someone who would engage in skywriting?" asks Sam.

"Possibly," says Andrews, closing the file and staring across the desk. "Look, I'm really busy tonight. If you want to look around and take some pictures of the raided areas, go ahead, but stay out of the way. Okay?"

"Right," says Sam, pushing his chair back and rising.

At least the trip won't be a total waste, you think, taking out your camera.

Andrews walks over to a map of the complex hanging on the wall. The map is dotted with small bulbs, apparently wired to a security system. Supply Warehouse Number 14 is marked with a red circle, and Andrews points out the easiest way to reach it without having to get past too many guards.

Suddenly the room is rocked by the high-pitched squeal of an alarm! You look at the map to see if Number 14 is being broken into, but it's the warehouse just south of it—warehouse Number 12. Andrews curses and heads for the door, shouting back, "If you want your story, keep close! Though with my luck, it'll be a false alarm!" The security chief goes through the door quickly, banging it open. Sam is hot on his heels, leaving you behind.

If you want to ditch Sam and try to change into Spider-Man to check out the alarm, go to **149**. If you want to check out the alarm as Peter Parker, turn to **141**.

160 *There's no way these five could have gotten back together,* you think, *even to kill me. That indicates a hoax, and Mysterio is a master of such illusions.*

You bound effortlessly over Kraven and land feet-first on Mysterio's fish-bowl helmet. The helmet shatters under the force of your blow, revealing a maze of wires beneath. The form of Mysterio crumples to the ground, but not before you lose 10 Health points from electrical damage. If your health has not failed you, move on to **145**.

161

You trust to the dark to mask your actions, and leap straight up in the air, reaching out to grab the side of the building with your patented wall-crawling touch.

Make an Agility FEAT roll. If the total is 12 or more, go to **5**. If it's 11 or less, turn to **99**.

162

You roll clear of the burning mass and rise slowly to one knee, coughing from the smoke. You look for anything else surviving the wreck, but see only a twisted mass of steel and burning circuitry. Proceed to **58**.

163

Electro! you think, swinging out into the night. *He's the key to the entire operation. Whoever stole the equipment probably was in cahoots with the master of electricity and busted him out only when everything else was in place.*

If Electro is working with another superpowered villain, there may be a leak in Project Pegasus security. You make a mental note to pass that on to Captain Nash, though it may have occurred to her already.

You retrace your path to where the Project Pegasus troopers were duking it out with Electro's mysterious allies earlier in the evening. The ruined armored car has already been pulled from the street, and traffic is flowing normally (for New York) past the alleyway.

The alleyway itself is no longer as empty as you remembered it. The Bureau of Public Works has set up a generator and equipment to clear away the debris kicked up by the explosion and make repairs. Signs warning "Men Working" are at both ends of the alley. You land atop one of the buildings overlooking the alley. The alleyway is singed darkly from the blast, more so toward the end where the Pegasus troopers were fighting.

What if, you wonder, *the purpose of the blast was to wipe out any trace of pursuit . . . if the men left behind were abandoned? Then that explosion might be more than just a going-away present. . . .*

You swing down to the alleyway itself.

Proceed to **26**.

164 The Battery-South Manhattan storage area is still a beehive of activity when you get there. In addition to the Con Ed security forces, there are representatives of the New York City Police Department present, and the area is ringed with police cars. It would be tricky to get into the place at this time.

Do you want to wait for the police to leave, or try some other approach? If you wish to wait, go to **180**. Otherwise, turn to **10** and make another choice.

165 The glow intensifies until you are standing in front of a pair of massive doors illuminated by a single powerful light. The trail through the slime ends here. To the right of the doors is parked a large hovercraft with a wide bed, suitable for carrying spools of wire.

the doors. *No welcome mat, though, and I bet this place isn't listed with Triple-A, either. Looks like I'll have to break in.*

You approach the huge metal doors. Do you want to try to force them open with your spider-like strength (turn to **61**), or investigate the situation further before acting (go to **110**)?

166

Interlude.

The criminal master of electricity wakes slowly. Does he detect something in the air? Yes, a knock-out gas was pumped into his cell. How long has he been out? Minutes? Hours?

Electro stretches, then realizes that his arms are no longer bound. He lashes out quickly, but finds his full reach blocked by a curved, smooth surface. He's enclosed in some kind of sphere! He hammers, but it won't break. If it's glass, it's the type they make aircraft windows out of.

His hammering produces a muffled ringing—and a response! He spots a light off to his right, a single bulb piercing his cage. Shadows move in front of the light. Where is he, anyway?

"Once more, my apologies," hisses a voice filled with malice. "It was necessary to drug you in order to make . . . final arrangements."

"What do you want?" asks Electro.

" 'Want' is a relative term," says the shadow, "as any student of psychology can tell you. Satisfy one want, and another comes to take its place. Ask instead, what is it I *need?*" He stresses the word *need* like a law professor making a point.

Electro remains silent, thinking. *Has he totally gone over the edge?*

The shadow continues. "*Need* is the operative word. I *need* to make myself a better person. I *need* to conquer my fears. To that end, you are going to help me conquer one of those fears—an accursed insect who has plagued both of our lives."

"Spider-Man?" asks Electro, still feeling around the sphere for an opening. There is a sharp hiss in answer to his question.

"Look," says Electro, "I can help you track down Spider-Man. I'll even go with you, if that's what you want. I hate that wall-crawler too, you know, so if—"

"Oh, yes," interrupts the shadowy figure.

"Hate. *Hate* is the right word for how I feel about that creature. And you *will* help me destroy him! You will help me in a fashion you cannot guess, without any chance of subversion or betrayal."

With that, an inhuman arm reaches for a massive switch. The lights come on around the room as the machinery starts up. Electro gets a full view of his prison, a clear ball of an insulated material supported in a massive collection of coils, generators, and wire. Far above him, nested at the highest point of the huge machine that entraps him, is the shadowy form of his captor. Electro cannot see his captor clearly from his prison, but he can feel the insanely evil grin, the eyes burning with hatred, as more switches are thrown and the machine throbs with an inhuman life.

The last of a series of switches is thrown, and corpulent fingers close around a large switch, pulling it down into a red-marked area on the gauge. Jets of electricity shoot through the glass ball, and Electro, who should be invulnerable to electricity, feels the pain, a tingling that shakes his entire body, almost tearing him apart.

Then comes the release of total darkness as his mind closes to the pain.

End of Interlude. Turn to **178**.

167

You are thrown off balance for a moment by your foe's appearance, and those few seconds cost you. The bolt of lightning arcs down and hits you square in the front. You shake with the force of the shock, and your health is reduced by 10 points. If your health is 0 or less, go to **187**.

If you are still intact, proceed to **67**.

168 You dodge most of the flaming debris and catch yourself on the wall. Subtract 15 points of Health. If your Health is now 0 or less, your adventure is over. Otherwise, turn to **2**.

169 *Ta-ta, Troopies,* you wave back at the forms of your inanimate playmates. *Let's reveal the puppeteer.*

This passage is similar to the previous one, dimly lit. At the end, you can see through an open door into a brightly lit room. From your far station, you can see some machinery. The smell of ozone is strong in the air. The walls of the passage are lined with wooden doors, and these are shut and have bars in the windows.

You are halfway down the hall when a low voice says, "Wait," in a short hissed tone. You see a hand wave at you from the bars.

Do you want to wait (proceed to **33**) or press on into the room (turn to **182**).

170 There is a sharp report of a rifle and a burning pain in your shoulder. You were so wrapped up in thought that you ignored your spider-sense until it was too late. Now badly injured, you desperately try to escape before you pass out.

There are other shots behind you, but none comes close, and you make it back over the fence. You make it one, two blocks, trying to websling with one arm. Your other arm tingles and feels numb.

Finally you pass out on a rooftop. You remember nothing beyond that point, but someone must have called the paramedics, because when you awaken you are resting comfortably in a hospital. No doubt the police are waiting outside your door to have a few words with you.

Your adventure ends here. You may start again, subtracting 1 point from your starting Karma.

171

There's no time to lose. As soon as the mugger is out of the alley, you're after him, not bothering to change into Spider-Man. You trust to the dark and confusion to keep your secret known.

Make an Intuition FEAT. If the total is 12 or more, go to **127**. If it's 11 or less, turn to **85**.

172

If you are still among the living, you land on your feet on the low concrete railing running around the Plaza. "Come on, Goblin, you've got to do better than that," you taunt.

If the Green Goblin hears you, he makes no reply. Meanwhile, your own mind is racing to determine who is behind that mask. *All of the Green Goblins have been talkative types, but this one is Silent Sam by comparison. Whoever he is, he's packing a wicked punch, and it's up to me to stop him!*

There is no time for further reflection because

the goblin glider is making a banking turn and will be coming back for another pass. Standing there in the clear is a great way to become roast Spidey. You can leap up to meet the Green Goblin's attack (turn to **184**), you can try to web the Green Goblin as he charges (proceed to **143**), or you can run from the Plaza, looking for someplace to hide (go to **82**).

173 You feel the explosion rather that hear it, as the figure that you assumed to be Doctor Octopus bursts open, with fire and twisted robotic parts flying everywhere. You don't sense anything for a long time except the feeling of swimming through dark waters before you finally come to.

You are in the street, surrounded by police officers and firemen. The firemen seem to have the blaze from the explosion under control. A police officer kneels down beside you.

"Spider-Man? Can you hear me?" he asks. You must have nodded, because he continues. "I'm afraid we're going to have to take you in for questioning on this one. The facility is pressing charges. You have the right to remain silent. You have the right to an attorney. If you cannot afford an attorney. . . ."

Blessedly, you fade out before he finishes reading you your rights.

Your adventure is over. You may begin again, using what knowledge you have learned so far to help make the correct choices. Subtract 3 Karma points from your initial total, though, to reflect the fact that you caused a major fire in South Brooklyn.

174

"What, may I ask, are you trying to do?" asks Andrews.

"Ouch," you say, flexing your gloved hands to see if anything is broken, "I was trying to get into the sewers below. I think that that is where your machinery went."

"So you were going to rip up my floor to do it, right?" notes Andrews. "Why can't you do things the simple way? There is a manhole somewhere around here. If there is a sewer running under this warehouse, we can get in that way."

After a search, you and Andrews locate a manhole and descend into the sewers. Go to **107**.

175

If it's Spider-Man they want, it's Spider-Man they'll get, you think, swinging across the city. *The only question is: Whom do I surrender to? The police? The city? Kingpin? The marines? The message in the sky was less than specific.*

Your path takes you into the Upper East Side of the city, near the borders of Carl Shurz Park. You look out over the park for a moment, then snap your fingers as it comes to you. *HE would know, or would know someone who would know.*

Go to **157**.

176

Interlude.

Deep beneath the city, a hovercraft settles to rest outside an entrance to an underground labyrinth unrecorded on any city maps. Two men, dressed in green uniforms, disembark, manhandling a bound human form between them, a form struggling in a bulky straitjacket. The pair and their prisoner approach the entrance, and a set of massive doors slides open to receive them.

The bound figure is not gagged, and his voice rings down the tunnels as his captors half-lead, half-carry him onward.

"Dolts!" shouts the captive. "Don't you realize who I am? Don't you know what I can do? I demand you turn me loose, fools! Now!" The captors make no acknowledgement of the figure's demand, but herd him through one more set of doors.

Max Dillon, called Electro by those who know and fear him, is pushed roughly through the doors into a small cell, empty save for a circle of bright light. His captors shove him harder than necessary, and he topples to his knees in the center of the light. The doors clank shut and lock behind him, and he is left alone. His solitude is broken by a crackling voice that erupts from a hidden loudspeaker.

"Welcome to my sanctuary, Electro," intones the voice. "I am sorry you had to receive such rough treatment at the hands of my men, but they were instructed not to let you out of your insulated straitjacket until we had had a talk. I have *need* of you, Electro—of you and of your special talents."

Electro blinks in the strong light for a moment, straining at his bindings.

"I—I know your voice!" he says, staggering to his feet. "I know you! Listen, we can work together! Between the two of us, we can recreate the Sinister Six!"

The only reply is a long, throaty laugh that reverberates in the cell long after the loudspeaker has been shut off.

End of Interlude. Turn to **8**.

177 "I don't know why you guys decided to hold a reunion," you say, "but I don't want to tackle you all at once."

You leap over Electro's head. Vulture wheels and turns toward you to intercept, while the others look on. Make an Agility FEAT to try to avoid Vulture. If the result is 16 or more, go to **70**. If the result is 12, 13, 14 or 15, go to **54**. If the result is less than 12, go to **148**.

178 "So, have you worked with Jameson long?" asks Karpierz as the two of you make your way through the *Bugle* building lobby.

"Years. Seems like centuries," you reply, still smarting from the verbal dressing down you received earlier.

"Figured as much," said Karpierz. "They only yell at who they think will let them get away with it."

"I take it you haven't worked for him before?" you ask, arching your eyebrows.

"First assignment. I was referred by another magazine."

"You'll learn," you say smiling, now the voice of experience. "He does that with everyone. It's his way of showing he cares."

Karpierz makes a muttering noise, then changes the subject. "You want to grab a cab," he says, "or take the IRT Lex, unless you have a car. . . ." His voice trails off as you walk out into unexpected darkness.

All over Manhattan, someone has turned off the lights.

Turn to **39**.

179 Make an Intuition FEAT roll. If your total is 16 or more, go to **91**. If it is less than 16, proceed to **140**.

180 *No use waiting on an empty stomach*, you think, swinging over to a local fast-food joint. A sleepy college student is at the fast-food window, paying attention to his books and not to the people at the drive-up window.

"Can I get an order to go?" you ask, dropping down over the edge of the building on a single webline.

"HellowelcometoMacBurgers. MayItake yourorder?" asks the youth without looking up.

"Two burgers, fries, and a cola," you say.

"Two MacBeefs, a MacDeepFat and a MacCola. Comes to $2.79," says the kid, still speaking into the mike. "Pleasedriveup."

You fish out the emergency money you keep in your belt and pay him. The student gives you your MacBurgers without looking up. "Thankyouand haveaniceday. Pleasecomeagain."

"Right," you say, shooting a webstrand up toward a nearby building and swinging off. *I wonder if he even noticed I was there? Great city, New York. Nothing fazes the natives.*

Go to **20**.

181

You wander around the perimeter of the warehouse, looking for anything to explain the missing spools of wire. There are no visible signs of entry in the walls, ceiling, or floor. If anything, it looks like the thieves tidied up before they left.

You get a dull buzzing in back of your mind as your spider-sense tries to warn you of something. Nothing seems imminently dangerous right now, but vaguely threatening, as if at a distance. It fades without further incident.

Sam Karpierz walks over to you. "Look, Pete," he says, "I'm going to be here trying to get something else out of old stoneface Andrews before my deadline. Why don't you get your pictures developed and we'll meet back at the *Bugle*?"

You agree quickly, realizing that gives you the chance to run down some leads of your own, concerning the thefts, Electro, and an unknown opponent who is fond of skywriting.

Turn to **111**.

182 *Not another one*, you think, walking past the cell door. *If I hit one more human-looking robot, I'll scream*. You walk down the remainder of the corridor and are brought up short at the entrance.

You are staring down the barrel of a huge weapon.

The room is filled by a massive machine that looks as if it was grown rather than constructed. Sparks dance along its sides, and at its center is Electro, glowing like a star and trapped in a glass bubble. Sitting atop that machine is Doctor Octopus, smiling. His human hand touches a button and a powerful bolt of electricity leaps towards you!

You dodge, making an Agility FEAT roll. Add Karma. If the result is 22 or more, go to **207**. If not, proceed to **38**.

183 Captain Nash sighs and begins to explain. She and her team were to escort Electro from his cell to a specially prepared holding area for his parole hearing tomorrow morning. While in transit, the team was ambushed by four individuals carrying electrical discharge guns. They opened fire as one, overturning the armored insulated car holding Electro and blowing off the rear doors. They then pinned down the Pegasus troops while two of the team went in and pulled Electro from the wreck. Electro was heavily sedated and, in addition, restrained by an insulated straitjacket.

Two of the team headed down the alley with the bundled Electro while their comrades kept Nash's troops pinned down with those Shock-zookas. By the time you arrived on the scene and drew their fire, the others had apparently escaped out the other side of the alley, but not before leaving an explosive package in the sewers, which, according to reports, Public Works is looking into as a cause for the blackout.

"Anyone see the goons leave with Electro?" you ask.

"We did a building-to-building search on the side of the alley with the New York Police Department, but it turned up nothing. They've vanished completely," she replies.

"How about the two goons I fought?"

"Resting comfortably," she says, stretching to relieve a neck cramp. "They were checked out for prior arrests, but they're small fry. They've been keeping pretty mum, but what we did get before their lawyers advised them to shut up was that Electro was the prize of the operation, but not the boss."

You nod and she continues, "The outfits look like those of HYDRA but are only imitations, according to a source at SHIELD. Talking to the people at SHIELD, by the way, was like pulling teeth; they know HYDRA is up to something, but they don't think they're connected with the kidnapping."

"So that leaves us with the question, where did they go?"

"Maybe the earth swallowed them," says Nash.

You smile beneath your mask. "Maybe it did, at that. I'm going to check out the scene of the crime. Maybe I'll find something else. Thanks, and I owe you a dinner." You head foı the window.

As you dive out into the night air, Nash shouts after you, "How about if you just bring back a pizza? I'll be here all night! And close the window after you, will you? There's a draft!"

Give yourself 1 additional Karma point for the lead and move on to **163**.

184 Before the rider of the Goblin Glider can fire another bolt, you are in the air. A quick somersault and you land square on the glider itself.

"I don't know who you are," you tell the Green Goblin, "but I'm going to take you out before you give me any further problems." Having said your piece, you swing a haymaker punch at your foe.

Make a Fighting FEAT roll. If you roll a 7 or less, go to **102**. If you roll an 8 or more, turn to **205**.

185 *Face it, hero,* you think as you sit on your perch above the city, *you're doing more harm than good. It's finally come to the point that someone hates you enough to endanger an entire city to get at you. The risks of being Spider-Man outweigh the value.*

You remove your mask and toss it out into the street far below. It flutters on the wind like a dark bat on the field of color beneath it. The rest of your costume follows, each piece dancing on the wind as it falls.

You change into your street clothes and examine your web-shooters. They have served you long and well, these trusty wrist-mounted devices. You crumple them up into a twisted ball of wreckage and consider tossing them over the side of the building as well. Thinking that, with your luck, they'd probably hit someone, you put the twisted mass of metal into your pocket.

The wind picks up and turns cold for a moment,

as if a great moment has passed. You think of other heroes who can act in your place. The city is crawling with them. One spider-bitten photographer more or less shouldn't make that much difference.

Seeing the last of your costume disappear in the lights below, you have the sudden urge to change your mind, to run down and retrieve your outfit and hunt down the villain who wants you out of the picture. *Too much risk there,* you reflect. *Whoever is behind this doesn't care if he brings an entire city to its knees. There's too much chance of innocent people getting hurt.*

Still thinking about your lost costume and the opportunities lost with it, you head for the rooftop door of the building. *Exit Spider-Man. I won't be missed,* you think glumly. The heavy metal door closes behind you with the harsh thump of a stone block laid over a crypt.

Your adventure ends here. You can start again if you wish, using whatever information you have learned so far, but you must reduce your Karma by 2 points.

186 *It should be relatively easy to modify a Hovercraft into a battering ram*, you think, trying to figure out which controls turn the darn thing on. *Trouble is, I'm a whiz at chemistry, but anything more complex than a motor scooter is beyond me.*

You are still pressing buttons and checking wiring when the massive doors slide open of their own accord, revealing a shadowy corridor beyond.

Hello, you think, abandoning your repair work and looking down the corridor. *Smile, you're on Candid Camera. I should have figured that the bright lights out here weren't just for valet parking. Apparently, my cordial "host" is watching, and doesn't like the idea of me wasting his precious Hovercraft on getting into his secret sanctum. Right sporting of him, eh what?*

You enter the complex cautiously, careful not to touch the metal doors. *Might as well have called ahead*, you think, moving into the corridor. *It's now or never.*

Go to **129**.

187

You feel as if you are swimming in a dark stream made of thick, black material, not water at all. Your confusion lasts for a moment, perhaps an eternity, then you regain consciousness.

Slowly you open your eyes. You are in an empty cell, lit by a single light. The cell has no door you can see, only four walls, a ceiling, and a floor, all made of a single solid stone. Up in the far corner of the cell is a camera lens and a loudspeaker.

The speaker comes alive with a crackle of static. "Welcome, my old foe," says a voice that you recognize in an instant. "I am so glad that I could bring you here. So . . . glad that I could finally defeat you outright. Don't bother to talk. I failed to equip your cell with listening devices. I did not want you to disturb me with your chatter."

You hurl a curse at your foe, his identity obvious to you now that you hear his voice. What he says is true, apparently, since the now-melodious voice just continues on. *Hope he can read lips,* you think.

"I want you to know how . . . happy I am to have you here. And you probably want to know what I intend to do with you. The answer is . . . nothing. Oh, I'll call you up and talk to you, but I have no inescapable deathtrap to trap you in. There is no air, water, or food in your cell, of course, but that should not prove to be a problem to Spider-Man . . . " The voice is cut short as you rip the loudspeaker and camera from the wall.

You sit down to examine the cell—to see how inescapable it really is. One wall seems to give a little, and with a lot of effort it may just give way and provide an escape. You silently curse the voice on the other side of the loudspeaker as you heave against the wall. You know who it is, and the next time you meet, the story will be different.

Your adventure ends here. You may start again, if you wish, reducing your initial Karma total by 2 points.

188 Using your skilled wall-crawling abilities, you move up the side of a building, leaping from roof to roof, making for warehouse 12, two down from the warehouse that has been robbed time and again. If there were any type of aircraft in the area, you would see them, but the skies are clear.

An ugly thought comes to your mind. Another of your old foes, Adrian Toomes, is an expert in electronics. He's also a flier. It was his electronic genius that let him create a flying harness that transformed him into the Vulture.

You stop for a moment, trying to shake this ugly thought from your mind. Vulture is as obsessed as Electro, and the two of them have worked side by side in the past. Still, how would that winged fiend lift that much material? Jewelry store heists are more in his line.

Your line of thought costs you as you are suddenly transfixed by a beam of light. Some sharp-eyed watchman has discovered you wall-crawling along in the darkness, and now other lights have you pinned down.

"Attention, Spider-Man," comes a rasping voice from below, amplified by a bullhorn. You recognize Andrews's voice. "You are trespassing on private property. Come down with your hands up." Your spider-sense is buzzing, and you can imagine half a dozen security guards releasing the safeties on their guns.

You can surrender to the guards or try to escape and find out who is really robbing Con Ed, who sprang Electro, and who wants you out of the way. They may not be the same person. If you surrender, go to **43**. If you try to escape, turn to **154**.

189

You walk to the doorway. Inside is a simple room, lit by a single gooseneck lamp on a modest desk. The light of the city outside pours through the venetian blinds of one window, forming a barred pattern of light and dark over a chair directly in front of the desk.

Behind the desk is a man. That is what your eyes tell you. A huge man dressed in white. Yet he seems larger than life in the gloom, wrapped in his power. He is Wilson Fisk, the Kingpin of Crime.

"Sit down, Spider-Man," he says in a flat, neutral voice. Your spider-sense is tingling mildly in the back of your brain, and for good reason: this man has threatened, on more than one occasion, to slay you.

"I'll stand," you say, trying to resist the urge to flinch in his presence. Fisk is seated, yet he looms in the room.

There is a silence. You begin again, "I'm here for . . ."

"Information," finishes the large man, "information concerning another of your foes, the one called Electro. Concerning the theft of goods from Consolidated Edison. Concerning a threatening message etched over the sky of my city."

His city, you muse. You say, "You know?"

"I know much of what occurs in the world around me," says Kingpin, rising and walking to the window. He pulls the blinds, letting the full light of the city, *his city,* flood into the room. "I do not like my world threatened."

There is another silence, the space of five heartbeats, as Kingpin surveys you and the room. "Your foe is threatening my world to get you. I do not like this. I want you to go to him. If you defeat him, my world will no longer be threatened. If you lose, I shall be rid of you. Either way, I will be stronger than I am now.

"But I am also a businessman, and would be akin to a fool to not take advantage of situations that fate may deal me." Kingpin smiles, the smile of a viper, not showing any teeth. "As a businessman, I feel I must add my own price to any benefits I may garner from the outcome of your little battle. A . . . commission, if you will. For services and information rendered."

"So?" you say. *Is the air conditioning on or has my blood turned to ice?*

"I want your word to aid me again," says Kingpin, "sometime in the future. Time, place, and favor unspecified. It may be illegal. It may be against your code. But I want that promise before you get your information."

You look at the fat man by the window long and hard. You are one of the "good guys," and as such honor your promises. Yet this man is as palpable an evil as you will find above or below street level.

Do you give your word to Kingpin in exchange for the information?

If you do, go to **4**. If you decline, turn to **97**.

190

"Obviously a phase-interrupted power oscillation," say Reed Richards, turning from his computer screen. "That's the only way such a blackout could be manipulated by present terrestrial technology without forcing a full shutdown in the Eastern power grid."

"Please, Professor Richards," you say, "slower and in English this time."

Reed Richards, leader of the Fantastic Four and one of the most brilliant scientists in the world, looks at you, then smiles. "Sorry," he says, "Johnny always says that I use ten words when two will do. What it means is that whoever is doing this is very, very good at it, and obviously has the best equipment available."

"What about the Con Ed thefts?" you ask.

"That's probably a part of it," responds Reed, "but your opponent would need more than just wires and equipment. For one thing, the power being used in his 'skywriter,' actually an electrostatic imprinter, would require a capacitator-transmitter the size of a small building. And despite my scans, I haven't been able to locate such a source."

"Okay," you say, sighing, "what about the list of charming fellows who would like to see me six feet under?"

"Well, most of your foes are in prison, though there are some that are still unaccounted for. Hobgoblin would be the one who could best do this type of manipulation, given his adaptation of the equipment, but the *modus operandi* is totally out of line. This could be the work of someone new. How about that Will O The Wisp character?

"Will O The Wisp isn't a criminal," you reply, "only a confused individual with a gigantic grudge against the Brand Corporation, which created him. I haven't seen him since that last go-around at Brand. He has the energy powers and can even pass through walls, but he's never tried anything like this. Tell you what, ask your computer to make a search assuming that all of my old foes are available for action. If that's true, then whodunnit?"

"Very well." Reed punches a few keys, and the computer spits out a couple of names. "The villain most likely to fight you in this fashion is none other than Doctor Octopus." The hero known as Mr. Fantastic is quiet for a moment.

"Doc Ock is in the loony bin," you say.

"Yes, South Brooklyn Psychiatric Facility," says Reed, a shadow passing over his face. "And his mechanical arms are incarcerated elsewhere. Still, it makes sense. Otto Octavius has a deep-seated hatred and fear of Spider-Man, made worse by repeated defeats at your hands." He shakes his head. "The computer indicated lesser chances for Shocker, Lightmaster, and Electro. By the way, didn't Electro just break out of prison earlier this evening?"

"Yeah. There's probably a connection, but I can't see him with this type of equipment."

"Nor I. There is the chance that he is working with someone else, however. Electro has worked with a number of other super-powered foes to take on our group as well as you."

"Uh-huh," you say, "a real team player." At this moment, a small red light flashes on the wall of the building.

"Hmm," say Richards, "a large artificial body is orbiting this location. This may or may not be connected with your problem. Do you want to help us check it out?"

If you wish to help Reed Richards examine the unidentified object, go to **130**. If not, say good-bye and move on to **197**.

191

You dodge the bolt at the last moment, but still feel part of the force of the blow. Take 5 points of damage. If your Health is 0 or less, go to **187**. If you can still shake your fingers and feel your toes, go to **172**.

192

Interlude.

"Be sure to secure him well," shouts a voice. "We'll be needing him quite soon, and we want him . . . well rested."

If the guards hear, they give no indication. They simply drag the form of Electro down a long hall toward his insulated cell. They wear heavily insulated green outfits, but the master of electricity doesn't seem to have any fight in him. He remains silent as they secure him in his cell.

Another prisoner is not so silent. As the guards

return to their posts, a dark-skinned arm reaches out from between the bars, snagging one guard's uniform.

"Please," says the voice within the cell, a voice low and urgent. "You've got to stop him!"

The guard says nothing.

"You realize he needs help," pleads the voice. "Even if he's paying you well, you must see that he's endangering millions to get one man."

The guard remains silent.

"You don't even have to be actively involved," says the voice. "Leave my door unlocked. I can go get help. He needs help, you know. If he goes through with his mad plan, there will be no stopping him. I know. I've . . . seen it happen before." His voice catches with emotion as he reaches out to the guard.

The guard removes the prisoner's hand with more than sufficient force and walks away.

"Please!" shouts the prisoner. "Let me talk to him at least!"

The guard says nothing, but down the hall from where Electro is imprisoned in huge, whirling machinery, there is an inhuman laugh, a laugh tinged with madness. HE has been listening, realizes the prisoner, and HE enjoys your discomfort. Realizing that he may have ruined any chance of detering HIM, the prisoner sits in his cell and weeps for his captor.

End of Interlude. Turn to **159**.

193

You look at the tattered shield, and think, *One more great idea hits the asphalt.* With the element of surprise lost, you can try the ventilators (go to **138**), or try to dodge your way past the death-bolt (move on to **86**). You know that you would have been slain by the force of the blow had it hit you directly, and only your insulative webbing reduced the shock. Give yourself 1 point of Karma.

194

You painfully pull yourself out of the bushes that you land in. The branches scratch you through your costume. *That's quite enough,* you think, approaching the burning pyre in the center of the courtyard. *I've had it with being blown up. You'd think someone like the Green Goblin would have more tricks up his sleeve than just trying to blow people up. . . .*

That last thought dies as you notice the wreckage of the glider and its rider. They were one machine, welded together and made of steel and chips. Your attacker was nothing more than a machine.

Proceed to **58**.

195

The floor of this warehouse is solid concrete three feet thick, designed to hold the heavy loads of massive machinery and equipment. Yet the wire spool is disappearing into it as if it were quicksand.

You can make a mental note to check out the floor of the warehouse later and reappear as Peter Parker before anyone notices you are missing, or you can go down to the floor of the warehouse and check out the phenomenon first hand. If you choose the former, go to **15**. If you choose the latter, turn to **204**.

196 *No chance to reach shore before it attacks,* you think quickly. *Have to fight it on its home turf. Alligator wrestling. Just like on TV.* The beast lunges at you through the water and is upon you.

Make a Fighting FEAT roll. If the result is a 9 or more, go to **35**. If the result is less than 9, go to **9**.

197 Choose the lead you want to follow and go to that number. You may be asked to return to this entry. Do not make the same choice twice.

You can:

1) Go to Ryker's Island. The federal prison located on this rocky outcrop in the East River is still the home of several of your old foes, and perhaps one of them has gotten loose without your knowing about it. Go to **94**.

2) See if Doctor Octopus is still under wraps. You remember that he is still being held for observation at a psychiatric facility in Brooklyn. Turn to **78**.
3) Check out the last known location of Electro, where the guys in green ambushed Project Pegasus. Go to **163**.
4) Try to get a line on the Vulture. Go to **200**.
5) Ask SHIELD, the super-spy organization, about HYDRA and AIM, criminal spy organizations. Turn to **83**.
6) Go ask the Fantastic Four about the blackout, the thefts, and the villains. Go to **190**.
7) Ask the Kingpin of Crime. As the most important single figure in the criminal underworld, the Kingpin may well know who is after you and why. Turn to **53**.
8) Go back to **137** and think of something else. Reduce your Karma by 1 point.

198

The UN Plaza is empty this time of night. The flags of the world's countries have been taken down, and most of the lights are out in the tall office section. You are alone and standing in the middle of the concrete. Not even the leaves are stirring.

"Ollie, Ollie Oxen-Free," you shout, hoping whoever is behind this bizarre attack will make himself known. "Wherever you are, here I am!"

There is silence for a moment, then the whirring of turbine engines somewhere near the river catches your ear. A dark shadow moves against the lights across the East River, and you see a bat-winged glider rise from the side of a courtyard overlooking the river. At first you think of your current foe, the Hobgoblin, but as the glider moves into the light, the colors of your opponent's outfit are clear: green and purple. *But that's impossible . . . ,* you think. *That is the costume of the Green Goblin!*

Your mind races as the figure approaches, the Green Goblin astride his turbine-powered Goblin-glider. *The original Green Goblin is dead,* you think, *the second, his son, cured of his delusion, and the third, the son's psychiatrist, slain in an explosion. Is there a fourth? Or is this some trick of the Hobgoblin or some other foe?*

"The Green Goblin lives!" shouts the airborne figure, the light reflecting on a face twisted with rage. "And Spider-Man dies!" he shrieks as he fires a bolt of lightning from his gloved hand.

Go to **6**.

199 *Dumb, Dumb, DUMB!* you think. *After all this dealing with electrical gear, I pull a bone-headed play like touching another metal door. Ouch!*

You reach out and grab the switch. Proceed to **153**.

200 *The great advantage of knowing your opponents on a first-name basis,* you think as you feed coins into a pay phone, *is that you can keep* *tabs on them whenever you need to.*

There is the metallic clicking of the phone gulping your money, the beeps and buzzes of the number you got from directory assistance, and the clicks of long-distance communication.

Finally a voice answers on the other end. "This is Adrian Toomes. I am not at home right now. Please leave a message and your number, and I will call you in the morning." Then a beep.

You hang up the phone in disgust. *What kind of message can I leave? "Hi, Vulture baby, this is Spidey. New York just got blotted out, and I was wondering if you knew anything about it. I'll be waiting at a pay phone, or you can call my Aunt May." Arrrrgggh!*

Okay, Vulture is still a suspect; what about the others? Turn to **197** and choose another option.

201

You leap up to where Doc Ock is standing and slam into him as hard as you can. Ock's mechanical arms react too late to protect him, and he collapses like a sack of wet laundry. The momentum of your leap carries the pair of you over the side the machine.

Your landing is not the gentlest in the world, and you have knocked Doc Ock out cold. *That's it?* you think. *One slug and he's out? After all the pain and agony he has caused, he's not going to fight one-on-one?* You pull back to hit him again, just in case he's playing possum.

"Stop!" shouts a voice from the chamber's entrance. Looking that direction for some new threat, you see a bespectacled black man leaning against the doorway: Doctor Jefferson, Doc Ock's psychiatrist. "Don't hit him! You fool!"

"Say what?" you snarl, backing off just a few feet in case Ock wants to use this distraction to his advantage. "Look, Doc, I've gone through Hades and high water because of this clown, and I'm going to see him defeated!"

"You defeated Otto the moment you escaped his trap," he says, walking over to where you and the mad doctor had sprawled. He checks Ock's pulse. "He'll live, but the damage may be insurmountable."

"The damage," you say, not in the mood to argue, "is already incredible. The madman was willing to threaten the entire island of Manhattan to get me."

"You may have done what you thought was right," retorts the Doctor, "but at what cost, my brash friend? Did you ever stop to think 'How will this madman react to being defeated and humiliated once again?' Have you stopped to consider what he will try next time, now that he has been trounced once more by an enemy who looms larger than life in his psyche? Did you stop to think beyond the point of, 'there's a bad guy, let's hit him?' "

You have no snappy answer for him, so the Doctor continues, in a softer voice. "Otto kidnapped me and left a robot duplicate in his place at the institute to bring me here, to show me he could face up to his fears and beat you. Conquer you. Conquer his fears. Yes, his methods were dangerously extreme, but so were yours in the end. Violence begets violence. Any hope I've had with months of analysis is reduced to nothing. We will have to begin again, prolonging the danger of him going on a mad terror spree. All because you thought with your fists."

Doctor Jefferson pauses, and the hum of Ock's machine can be heard. "You have saved the city, young man, and for that everyone should be grateful, but you should try to be less . . . violent next time."

You want to argue with the man but can't, and so you exit the way you came in, leaving Dr. Jefferson to call the authorities. *I should be feeling like a hero, but instead I feel like a heel. Maybe next time I'll try to think first, then strike out.*

At least we'll have a next time, you think. *Jefferson can moan about the lost opportunities, but the fact remains that the madman was a danger, not only to me, but to himself, his psychiatrist and the city at large—Manhattan, Con Ed, the* Bugle . . .

You slap your forehead with the palm of your hand. *The Bugle*! I promised to get that film in for Sam's report! Kate Cushing will have my guts for garters if I mess up again. The fact that none of this would be a worry if Ock succeeded is immaterial. The city lives, and with it comes all the daily responsibilities . *Now I HAVE to find a way out of this sewer. Life goes on, and I have to keep trying.*

And trying seems to make all the difference.

202 You and Sam stay close together as you leave the building. The initial panic seems to have subsided slightly. Already some of the windows are lit by candles and weak private generators. There is a regular staccato of shouts and the occasional sound of breaking glass, but the crowds seem more confused than angry. Undoubtedly some criminals will seek to use the darkness to fatten their pockets. You consider ditching Sam for a moment and going off as Spider-Man, but you decide against that. Unless you see something that really requires your presence, you're going to stay Peter Parker for a while.

You decide to take some pictures. A couple of fires have been started in trash bins and people are gathering around them, more for the light than the heat. Street vendors selling glow-in-the-dark hats, candles, and flashlights are doing a landslide business. Police are on the street, maintaining a high profile of visibility to ease the crowd and to try to unsnarl the traffic jams at every major intersection. Sam stops people and asks questions. You can see that he has another story in mind other than the electrical equipment thefts. *Could the two be connected?* you wonder.

You and Sam grab hot dogs and sodas from a vendor, his stand bathed in pale green light from fluorescent tubes powered by a small generator. The hot dogs look fleshy brown under the light.

"I was wrong," says Sam between bites.

"About what?" you ask.

"About the cascade effect," he says. "The entire eastern seaboard should be out if that happened. I've been talking to people who've made their way down from upper stories, and they've seen the lights on in Brooklyn, Queens, even Jersey. Portable radio report confirms it. It's just Manhattan that's out."

"You got a theory?"

"Nope," he says, slurping down the rest of his cola. "It should be like I described it. You can't just take Manhattan out of the circuit without a lot of power going out elsewhere. Where could that much power go?"

The answer comes in a flash of light that illuminates the street like a fireball, bathing the crowd in a harsh white glare.

"It's that darned Fantastic Four," mutters the hot dog vendor. "One of their bunch is a human fireball, you know."

"Torch," you correct. "Human Torch. And it's not fire. It's lightning. LOOK!" You point at the sky.

Turn to **13**.

203

"I thought you'd gone straight, Sandy, but I've been wrong before," you say, leaping feet-first at the silent Sandman. You know Sandman can make his body as resistant as sand or as hard as a rock, so you leap feet-first at him, hoping to follow up with your fists.

You meet a different kind of resistance than you are expecting, however. As your feet make a solid contact, a staggering electrical shock runs through your body. *Is Electro giving lessons to his friends?* you wonder. Go to **208** to check out the damage done.

204 You drop down to floor level on a single strand of webbing from right above the rapidly disappearing spool of wire. Landing on the top of the spool, you find the wire solid enough. Your added weight doesn't seem to speed up its sinking into the concrete.

Like quicksand, you think as more of the spool slowly disappears beneath the surface of the concrete, leaving nary a ripple. *I hope that there's something under there that I can sink into. Otherwise, I'm soon going to become a spider in cement!*

You take a deep breath as the last of the wire vanishes beneath your feet, hoping to follow the wire down into the earth. To your surprise, you don't sink into the cement. Instead, the concrete feels hard under your bare feet.

Bare feet? you think. You lift one foot. The uniform's still there, but it feels as if you're walking barefoot on the concrete.

Outside you hear the crackle of a bullhorn, then Andrews's voice: "Attention in the warehouse! You are trespassing on private property and have two minutes to give yourselves up at the main door."

It's time for a little experiment. You fish out one of your spare web-packets from your belt and lower it to the concrete. The web-packet sinks into the concrete up to where your fingers are holding it, then stops. The concrete around the half-immersed web-packet feels smooth to the touch.

Okay, what would Reed Richards make of this? you think, pulling the packet out of the cement. *Some sort of illusion? A selective force field? Some kind of phasing power, like Shadowcat of the X-Men? Except this time, only the field is selective.* You're not sure if even Shadowcat can pull off that yet.

Suddenly you hear a rattling at the door. Either you've spent too much time thinking about it, or Andrews's men are jumping the gun. It wouldn't be good public relations for Spidey to be found on the scene instead of the missing supplies, so you leap for your web-strand and crawl up to the skylight, pulling the strand up behind you just as Andrews, Karpierz, and a dozen gun-toting guards burst in.

Exit Spidey, re-enter mild-mannered Peter Parker, you think, moving back to where you stashed your clothes. *I'll make my excuses to Karpierz and investigate this further*, you think. Add 1 point of Karma to your score for your discovery.

Slipping away to rejoin the others is as easily said as done. Sam is trying to corner Andrews in a quote and merely nods when you suggest that you meet back at the *Bugle*. The guards are searching for any type of secret passage by which the material could have been transported.

Andrews is saying something about three feet of solid concrete beneath them when you leave. But you'll be back.

Go to **111**.

205 You strike the Green Goblin square in the face with a powerful blow, and are startled by the results. The face mask of your foe breaks away, as it is little more than a covering for what lies below. Lifelike eyes look at you from within a maze of wiring and circuitry, and where the mouth should be, there is nothing more than a speaker grid. Smoke begins to pour out of the sides of the Green Goblin's head.

"Now, Spider-Man," says the speaker, crackling as small flames appear around the neck, "you will perish with me." The turbine of the goblin glider speeds up and the pair of you go into a power dive, heading straight for the ground!

Make an Agility FEAT roll. If the result is 13 or less, go to entry **51**. If the result is 14 or more, turn to **124**.

206 *I feel like a Peeping Tom*, you think as you scrabble from window to window. *The highest security area is on the top floor. My best bet is to start there*. Reduce your Karma total by 1 point.

As carefully as you can, you examine the windows. You look in on three sleeping patients and one pacing the floor before you find Doc Ock's room. Through the bars of the window, you see him sitting on his bunk in a lighted room. He seems to be staring straight ahead blankly.

Otto Octavius, without the many-tentacled harness that he wears about his waist as Doc Ock, is anything but an imposing figure—short and pudgy, dressed in institutional greens, and wearing tinted lenses. An uninformed observer would be surprised that this man is a master at radiation research and even more surprised to know that, when his tentacle-like arms are attached, he is the madman known as Doctor Octopus.

You feel a pang of pity for him. It was an accident that gave him his powers and unbalanced his mind, but it was his continual defeats at your hands that brought him to his present situation.

As if he senses your thoughts, Octavius's head

swivels to meet your gaze. No, not quite meet it, but look past it, as if you aren't even there. He's looking at you but not reacting.

Do you want to pull off the grillwork and enter the room, or leave Otto be? If you decide to enter, go to **29**. If you elect to leave Otto in peace and try something else, turn to **197**.

207 You nimbly dodge the lightning-like beam and the entire wall behind you shakes as the full force of the power that lights Manhattan rattles the entire complex.

If that hit, you think, shocked by the power of the blow, *there wouldn't have been enough of me to mail home. Doc is crazy, and overreacting. He's using a sledgehammer to kill a spider!*

You handspring across the room and land on the side of Ock's machine, the one place where his ray cannot hit you. Turn to **113**.

208 You slam into your opponent with all your might but are shocked backwards by a powerful electrical force that courses through you the moment you touch him. Take 10 points of damage in the process, and reduce your Karma total by 1 point. Your opponent, on the other hand, looks unharmed and has not uttered a word since you entered the room. *Not a talkative bunch. What's the matter?* you ponder.

Time to check out your options. You can run (turn to **120**). You can jump over your opponents to reach the far side of the room (turn to **177**). You can use your webbing against them. Or, you may choose to fight any of your remaining foes: Electro (turn to **21**), Sandman (go to **203**), Vulture (go to **63**), Kraven (go to **95**), or Mysterio (go to **160**). You know that an attack similar to the one you just made will only end in similar results.

209

Your mind races as you cling to the side of the machine. Above you, Doctor Octopus looks stunned by your escape, yet already his tentacle-like arms are squirming, twisting knobs and throwing switches.

I've fought Doc Ock almost all my crime-fighting career, you realize. *Yet every time I've defeated him, he's come back angrier. I could fight him and win, but what about next time? Is violence the only way to deal with this madman?*

Small panels open in the sides of the machine,

and wicked-looking blasters emerge. *If I'm going to make a play, it's now or never,* you realize. *Another moment and it's back to slugfest city.*

"Doc?" you shout over the crackling din. "How about if we just talk?"

"Talk?" sneers Doctor Octopus, his face contorting in a hideous grimace. "You mean plea for my mercy? Or is this one of your contemptible jokes?"

Well, no one said this was going to be easy, you think.

"No, just talk," you say aloud. "No snappy quips. No insults. No threats. Just talk."

The air crackles, and the smell of ozone is strong in the air. You note from the corner of your eyes that the blasters are pointed directly at you, but Ock has made no motion to fire them.

"Talk, wall-crawler," says Doctor Octopus, his voice more curious than angry.

So far, so good, you think.

"I want you to think about what happened in the city. The blackout. All the confusion. People got hurt, Doc . . . Otto. People who don't know you or me. Innocent folks. I know you don't care about me, but I'm worried about them. I'm worried about you, too." You cross your gloved fingers and hope.

"Worried?" Doctor Octopus echoes your words, but his features start to soften. His hand rests on the firing button, but he doesn't press it.

"Yes, worried—really," you continue. "You were . . . are . . . a great scientist. A genius, Otto. Yet all this . . ." You wave an arm at the gadget-filled room. "All the threats and hurting people. Do I frighten you this much?"

For a moment, the old rage seems to come over

Ock's face, and you tense to spring out of the way if he hits the blasters. Then, with an equal suddenness, his face goes calm. Revelation? Reason?

One more push, you think.

"I want to help you, Otto. If hurting me will do it, I'll stand here and let you blast me. Let me help you . . . please."

That proves to be the deciding blow. Octopus's madness seems to disappear, the hatred draining from his face. His hand pulls back from the button, his shoulders slump, and his mechanical arms retract.

"I . . . I didn't mean . . . I'm sorry. I'm just so . . . frightened." He buries his face in his hands.

You let out a sigh of relief. *He's just scared,* you think. *That's what this is all about. All the robots and blasters and weapons, simply because he's scared!*

You stay with Octopus until the authorities arrive to take him and Electro into custody. Doctor Jefferson, the psychiatrist Ock kidnapped, approaches you. "I want to thank you for your help, Spider-Man. You succeeded where I failed. But I wonder about something. Why did you try to help, when in the past you and Otto always fought?"

"Sometimes," you say, "having great power is knowing when *not* to use it. Hitting Ock would just mean he'd be meaner the next time. You'll have to help him as best as you can."

"I will," says the psychiatrist, nodding. "We're all lucky to have your help, no matter what the *Bugle* says."

You slap your forehead with your hand. "The *Bugle!*" you cry. You still have to get those pictures turned in, or Cushing will have your hide.

"Sorry to just chat and run, Doc, but you've reminded me of another engagement. See you in the funny pages."

You don't wait for an answer, but instead swing off into the night. Before you, the city is spread out in a tapestry of light. You've defeated a deadly foe by helping, not hurting. Now if only Jameson would be as understanding. . . .

You laugh, launch into a somersault, and send another web-line into the night.

Richard Carpenter's
ROBIN OF SHERWOOD

Gamebook 1:
THE KING'S DEMON
Graham Staplehurst

Have you ever wondered what it was like to be Robin Hood, outlaw and protector of Sherwood Forest? Well, here's your chance to find out. In this gamebook YOU are Robin of Sherwood, son of Herne the Hunter, champion of the poor and oppressed. As you go through the book you make your own choices and use your skill and judgement to outwit your old enemy, the corrupt Sheriff of Nottingham and his loathsome, bullying servant, Sir Guy of Gisburne.

Gamebook 2:
THE SWORD OF THE TEMPLAR
Paul Mason

In this gamebook, the peace of the forest you love and the lives of your companions are in danger. Your enemy is a Knight Templar, Sir Roger of Ledbury, and the force he wields threatens the very existence of Herne the Hunter! Why does the Knight Templar so desire your downfall? Will you be able to prevent him from achieving his goal, or has Robin of Sherwood met his match? Even with your sword Albion at your side, you will need all your strength and resourcefulness to meet this challenge!

Fighting Fantasy Gamebooks

1. THE WARLOCK OF FIRETOP MOUNTAIN
2. THE CITADEL OF CHAOS
3. THE FOREST OF DOOM
4. STARSHIP TRAVELLER
5. CITY OF THIEVES
6. DEATHTRAP DUNGEON
7. ISLAND OF THE LIZARD KING
8. SCORPION SWAMP
9. CAVERNS OF THE SNOW WITCH
10. HOUSE OF HELL
11. TALISMAN OF DEATH
12. SPACE ASSASSIN
13. FREEWAY FIGHTER
14. TEMPLE OF TERROR
15. THE RINGS OF KETHER
16. SEAS OF BLOOD
17. APPOINTMENT WITH F.E.A.R.
18. REBEL PLANET
19. DEMONS OF THE DEEP
20. SWORD OF THE SAMURAI
21. TRIAL OF CHAMPIONS
22. ROBOT COMMANDO
23. MASKS OF MAYHEM
24. CREATURE OF HAVOC
25. BENEATH NIGHTMARE CASTLE
26. CRYPT OF THE SORCERER
27. STAR STRIDER
28. PHANTOMS OF FEAR
29. MIDNIGHT ROGUE

FIGHTING FANTASY – The Introductory Role-playing Game
THE RIDDLING REAVER
OUT OF THE PIT – Fighting Fantasy Monsters
TITAN – The Fighting Fantasy World

Steve Jackson's
SORCERY!

1. The Shamutanti Hills

Your search for the legendary Crown of Kings takes you to the Shamutanti Hills. Alive with evil creatures, lawless wanderers and bloodthirsty monsters, the land is riddled with traps and tricks waiting for the unwary traveller. Will you be able to cross the hills safely and proceed to the second part of the adventure – or will you perish in the attempt?

2. Kharé – Cityport of Traps

As a warrior relying on force of arms, or a wizard trained in magic, you must brave the terror of a city built to trap the unwary. You will need all your wits about you to survive the unimaginable horrors ahead and to make sense of the clues which may lead to your success – or to your doom!

3. The Seven Serpents

Seven deadly and magical serpents speed ahead of you to warn the evil Archmage of your coming. Will you be able to catch them before they get there?

4. The Crown of Kings

At the end of your long trek, you face the unknown terrors of the Mampang Fortress. Hidden inside the keep is the Crown of Kings – the ultimate goal of the *Sorcery!* epic. But beware! For if you have not defeated the Seven Serpents, your arrival has been anticipated . . .

Complete with all the magical spells you will need, each book can be played either on its own or as part of the whole epic.